COPING WITH STRESS:
A GUIDE TO LIVING

More than 80 Wiley Self-Teaching Guides teach practical skills from math to microcomputers, popular science to personal finance. STGs on business and management skills include:

ACCOUNTING ESSENTIALS, Margolis
*ASSERTIVE SUPERVISION, Burley-Allen
BEYOND STRESS TO EFFECTIVE MANAGEMENT, Gmelch
BUSINESS MATHEMATICS, Locke
BUSINESS STATISTICS, 2nd ed., Koosis
CHOOSING SUCCESS: HUMAN RELATIONSHIPS ON THE JOB, Jongewald
COMMUNICATING BY LETTER, Gilbert
COMMUNICATION FOR PROBLEM-SOLVING, Curtis
CREATIVE COST IMPROVEMENT FOR MANAGERS, Tagliaferri
GMAT: GRADUATE MANAGEMENT ADMISSION TEST, Volkell
*HOW TO READ, UNDERSTAND, AND USE FINANCIAL REPORTS, Ferner
IMPROVING LEADERSHIP EFFECTIVENESS: THE LEADER MATCH CONCEPT, Fiedler
LISTENING: THE FORGOTTEN SKILL, Burley Allen
LSAT: LAW SCHOOL ADMISSION TEST, Volkell
MANAGEMENT ACCOUNTING, Madden
MANAGING BEHAVIOR ON THE JOB, Brown
MANAGING THE INTERVIEW, Olson
MANAGING YOUR OWN MONEY, Zimmerman
MEETINGS THAT MATTER, Hon
PERFORMANCE APPRAISAL: A GUIDE TO GREATER PRODUCTIV-ITY, Olson
QUANTITATIVE MANAGEMENT, Schneider
QUICK LEGAL TERMINOLOGY, Volkell
QUICK MEDICAL TERMINOLOGY, Smith
QUICK TYPING, Grossman
QUICKHAND, Grossman
SKILLS FOR EFFECTIVE COMMUNICATION: A GUIDE TO BUILDING RELATIONSHIPS, Becvar
SPEEDREADING FOR EXECUTIVES AND MANAGERS, Fink
SUCCESSFUL SUPERVISION, Tagliaferri
SUCCESSFUL TIME MANAGEMENT, Ferner
USING GRAPHS AND TABLES, Selby
USING PROGRAMMABLE CALCULATORS FOR BUSINESS, Hohen-stein

Look for these and other Wiley Self-Teaching Guides at your favorite bookstore!

*In preparation

COPING WITH STRESS:
A GUIDE TO LIVING

James W. Mills, Ph.D.
Drew University
Madison, New Jersey

John Wiley & Sons, Inc
New York • Chichester • Brisbane • Toronto • Singapore

To
Connie, Thelma, Richard, Robert, Joyce

Library of Congress Cataloging in Publication Data:

Mills, James Willard, 1937–
   Coping with stress.

   (Wiley self-teaching guides)
   Includes index.
   1. Stress (Psychology)   I. Title.
BF575.S75M54   1982   158'.1   82–16044
ISBN 0–471–87678–X

Printed in the United States of America

   10   9   8   7

CONTENTS

PREFACE

This relatively brief, action-oriented, practical guide is designed to give the reader specific methods for reducing and controlling stress in one's life. My experience in counseling and in working with stress management groups has convinced me that *talking about stress control is not enough: people want to learn what they can do about their stress and how to do it.* The guide briefly describes twenty specific methods of stress management which have been developed by experts through years of clinical practice and empirical research. They are the means by which people can deal with the types of stress associated with everyday living.

Each method is accompanied by an exercise or exercises which give the reader practice in stress control. Completion of the exercises not only enables readers to understand how to work on stress but also helps make the methods part of their thinking so that they can be recalled when stress is experienced. Frequently people learn about stress management in one context but forget it when they experience stress in a different context. My students over the years have told me that completion of the exercises makes the methods more readily available when needed. *By moving immediately from general discussion to specific action, the exercises enable the readers to incorporate the methods into their thinking and, therefore, to apply them when they encounter stressful situations.* (Please note that space for answers has been left in the exercise sections, but readers are advised to use a separate sheet of paper if additional space is required.)

The exercises and the discussion of methods, while presented together, can to some extent be utilized independently of each other. Some readers, for example, may want to work on some of the exercises before they read the discussion of the principles. In dealing with groups, sometimes the application of particular methods to a specific stressful situation effectively prepares the way for the discussion of that method. Thus this guide is not intended as an outline to be followed slavishly, but as a flexible tool which respects the reader's need to use it appropriately in his/her own unique circumstances.

Designed for people who would like to do something about stress in their lives, the guide can be used by individuals and in groups. Anyone experiencing stress can use the guide. Those who work closely with others, such as teachers, youth workers, clergypersons, and counselors, can also make use of this guide, since the methods presented here are easily taught to others. Stress management groups in colleges, churches, industry, and other settings will find that when small groups of people work on the exercises together, interesting and useful discussions follow easily.

In order to be as brief and practical as possible, I have omitted long academic discussions and have not presented the numerous research findings which support the suggestions given here; I save that for the classroom. I have also tried to limit the scope of the guide to a focus on stress control. This is not intended as a book on interpersonal relations, personal growth, or group dynamics. When appropriate, the reader is referred to other sources when the discussion begins to move from stress management to another, more general area. Thus, the guide suggests that making physical health a priority is useful in a stress management program and then suggests that the reader look elsewhere for details of a physical health program. In particular, since the guide deals with the stresses of daily living, it is not intended as a cure-all for every personal problem and is not a substitute for personal counseling or psychotherapy when these are appropriate.

Finally, the guide uses such terms as *control, manage,* and *deal with* your stress. Stress is a part of life and while we can deal with it, we can never hope to eliminate it completely.

Three friends deserve special thanks for their help in preparing this guide. My colleague, Phil Jensen, read and critiqued the rough draft of the manuscript. Deborah Penner, my academic assistant, prepared the three descriptions of people in stressful situations which appear in the unit on applying the methods. Renee Caffrey managed to type the manuscript in much less time than I had thought possible. She also took a personal interest in the manuscript, offered a number of very helpful suggestions, and eased my work considerably. I thank these friends for helping make this guide possible.

James W. Mills

INTRODUCTION

WHAT IS STRESS?

What would you say if you were asked to describe your most recent experience of stress? You would probably tell of experiences such as these:

- Your sense of being rushed and hassled because you have a great deal of work to do in a limited amount of time
- Your anger at getting caught in a traffic jam
- Your worry about not having enough money to pay your bills
- Your frustration when learning that you can't go on the vacation you had planned
- Your annoyance at your children for making so much noise while playing upstairs
- Your anxiety about your school exam.

Stress is our inner reaction to things that happen to us and demands that are placed on us. We experience stress when we are anxious, worried, ashamed, or angry, whether the source of our feeling is ourselves, some other person, or something that happens to us. We can deal with stress adequately only when we consider both components of stress: the external events and demands in our lives and our inner reaction to them.

People sometimes limit their view of stress to the stressor or the external part of stress. They see stress as the work they have to do, the demands of their employer, the actions of other people, and difficult situations (for example, traffic jams, illness, or uncomfortable personal relationships). This way of looking at stress is incomplete because it locates stress outside of the person and implies that a given event is stressful for everyone. We all know that isn't true. If someone asked you to give a talk before a local political organization, you might find that a very stressful demand. Someone else would be delighted to give such a talk. The sound of a television playing loudly in another room may be very distressing to one person and of no consequence to another. Stress occurs only when our inner reaction to these events is one of discomfort or displeasure.

We also need to recognize that the demands placed on us are not always external demands. You may be stressed because of the many things you have to do at work, but much of your stress may come more from demands you place on yourself than from those placed by your employer. People often increase their stress by asking much more of themselves than others ask of them. A woman who expects to please her husband at all times or a student who insists on getting an A on every exam will experience more stress than others with more realistic expectations.

You may have heard it said that stress is not necessarily bad for us and that it can even be good for us. Some people seem to thrive on stress—they respond to the many demands in their lives with enthusiasm and energy. We think of an athlete who strains to win the contest or the businessperson who welcomes the challenge of competition. Getting married is stressful, but we welcome that stress! As we work on controlling our stress, we need to avoid confusing stress with challenge, excitement, and motivation. This guide views stress as our unpleasant, unwanted inner reaction to events and demands in our lives. It is true that stress in the more general sense can be good for us, but since most people, when they complain about stress in their lives, are using the term in its negative sense, that will be the focus of this guide.

Many books limit their discussion to the *physical* experience of stress, such as tenseness, high blood pressure, and hypertension. This guide considers emotional reactions as important as physical ones because when people seek help with their stress they speak more of their feelings than of their physical reactions. Further, the emphasis on the physical experience often results in discussing only those stress control methods aimed at that experience, including relaxation and biofeedback. While these methods are very valuable, a more complete program of stress management makes use of many others. This guide reviews methods of dealing with stress that deal with both the physical and emotional parts of our inner reactions.

WHAT IS THE SOURCE OF STRESS AND STRESS CONTROL?

Since stress consists of our inner reaction to events and demands, we can see that stress has two primary sources: events and demands in our lives and our inner reaction to them. Stress has its source both outside us, for example, in the work we have to do, and within us, as in our response to work. The management of stress, therefore, involves working with ourselves as well as with the events and demands facing us. However, since we can usually deal more effectively and practically with our thinking and our reactions than with the events and demands themselves, this guide focuses chiefly on how we can manage our reactions to those events and demands.

Most of us have a natural tendency to seek the answer to stress reduction outside of ourselves. We believe that we would suffer less stress if only we had a different job, if our spouse or friends would behave differently, or if our circumstances were somehow different. All of that may be true—and we should change circumstances whenever we can. But frequently that is not possible. Further, some people have patterns of thinking, habitual reactions to situations, and general feelings about themselves such that they experience stress in almost any circumstance. Hoping that a change in our circumstances will reduce our feelings of stress is a passive approach.

HOW CAN I GET THE MOST OUT OF THIS GUIDE?

First, decide that you are going to manage stress. Harold Greenwald in his book *Direct Decision Therapy* states that after years of experience he concluded that the most important thing he did as a therapist was to help people convert a *wish* to change into a *decision* to change. It's easy to wish that things were different. It's easy to fantasize that we are great at handling stress. But wishing and fantasizing aren't enough. Greenwald's comment on therapy applies to all attempts to improve ourselves: we must consciously and thoughtfully *decide* that we are going to manage our stress. Dozens of books have been written on how to diet and some people read one after another without benefit. Why? Often because they have not really *decided* to lose weight. They *want* to lose weight but they have not really *decided* to lose weight. They have not decided to take the time and effort involved in any weight-reduction program.

There is an old proverb: Some people want to go to heaven; others want to hear ten lectures on how to go to heaven. It is easier to hear another lecture or read another book than it is to decide to do something specific about our situation. If you are to manage stress in your life, decide now that you will take the time and effort involved. There are no magic answers.

Second, read all the way through this book. This guide is not very long. You can read it in a short period of time. Read through all the methods and browse through the exercises so that you become familiar with the entire program of stress control. The methods are designed to interact with and complement one another; so it is a good idea to have a general idea about all of them before studying any one in detail. Once you have done this, you may choose to work through each method in the order presented or to study those methods that seem most useful to you regardless of their position in the text.

Third, do the exercises. Learning a method of stress control is one thing; applying it is another. The exercises are designed to show you how to apply the methods. In teaching stress management in the past, I have learned that telling people what to do is not enough. People do not benefit from being told, for example, to seek support; they need to be shown just what that means and how they might do it. The exercises in this guide offer a simple, practical way of learning to use the methods of controlling stress. By moving you from a general discussion to specific action, they enable you to incorporate the methods into your thinking and then to apply them when you encounter stressful situations. These exercises were developed over the past several years of teaching a course on stress management. I found that students gained much more from the course after I introduced these exercises, and their comments have helped me improve them. Resist the temptation to skip over the exercises as mere busywork.

Some of the methods discussed here might seem to be stating the obvious, prompting you to say, "Everyone knows that." You may be right. But it's amazing how much difficulty we get into by forgetting the obvious. Other methods might seem trivial or mechanical: I had that reaction myself when I first studied them. Now, the more I work with people and stress control, the more I find that what seemed trivial or mechanical at first turned out to be very useful in the long run. So remember, only by practicing these methods in the exercises can you appreciate their full value.

Fourth, develop a plan of action. Once you have learned and practiced methods of stress management, the crucial next step is to utilize them in your own life. It won't do you much good to read the methods and do the exercises, and then forget about it all. Think carefully about how you can utilize each method in your daily living. Actually, the exercises help you do this, since most of them are implementations of the methods. Nevertheless, you will need to think beyond the text and exercises and consider ways of making methods of stress management part of your approach to stressful situations in your life.

Fifth, use judgment. This guide describes a number of methods to control stress and discusses some of the ways they can be used. The exercises provided for each method can help you know when and how to apply them in specific situations. Obviously, not every method for dealing with stress is appropriate for every situation or person. You must use your own judgment in selecting which methods to use and when to use them. For example, the guide teaches us both to tolerate uncertainty and reduce uncertainty. The more uncertain we are in a given situation, the more stressed we are likely to be (see Method 17, "Reduce Uncertainty"). Thus, we can reduce stress by reducing uncertainty. However, sometimes we can't do that: there are situations when we will have unanswered questions no matter what we do. At such times, we are better off to learn to tolerate uncertainty (Method 9) than to attempt further reduction of uncertainty.

Similarly, the guide suggests that you learn to assume control as a way of dealing with stress (Method 16). Generally, the more we feel in control, the less we are stressed. Nevertheless, there are times when we feel better because we have no control in a situation. For some people being in control means assuming responsibility—and they may feel better when they aren't responsible. Perhaps there are times when you felt relief when you turned a task over to someone else. At such times you felt better not assuming control. Likewise, while Method 19 explains how too much or too rapid change can be stressful and that we can reduce stress by minimizing change, there will be times when we are stuck in a routine and need more change. At such times we might employ Method 6A, "Change Your Environment."

Sixth, use a combination of methods. While each of the methods discussed in this guide can be helpful by itself, you can help deal with stress when you use a combination of methods. Fortunately, a single action that you take may utilize several methods at one time. When a person faces a new, unfamiliar task about which he or she knows little and talks about this with a friend to learn what must be done, that person is taking a problem-solving approach (Method 3), reducing uncertainty (Method 17) assuming control (Method 16), and utilizing resources (Method 20C). While each method is discussed separately to enable you to understand its unique contribution to stress control, in actual life situations, several methods operate at one time.

Now that you understand how the term *stress* is used in this guide and are familiar with the six ways to get the most out of this guide, you are ready to review the basic methods of stress control. These methods are divided into four major categories. The first set of methods, GETTING READY, enables you to prepare for stress management by taking inventory and viewing stress in a more helpful way. You work on your thinking about and reactions to stress in the second set of methods, WORKING ON YOURSELF. Those steps we can take to modify the task facing us constitute category three, WORKING ON THE TASK. In addition to working on ourselves and our task, we can reduce the stress we experience by obtaining support. This very important method is discussed in Part IV, WORKING ON THE ENVIRONMENT.

PART I

GETTING
READY

How do we begin a stress management program? People who successfully control their stress approach their day-to-day living with healthy attitudes toward their daily tasks, stressful situations, and themselves. They look at stressful situations as a challenge for action. They work to resolve, rather than automatically react against, their problems and difficulties. They see themselves as growing, developing people who can make the most out of any situation. Part I of this guide helps you become aware of the stress in your life and then introduces you to the attitudes and approaches toward stress which are the basis for successful stress management.

METHOD 1

TAKE INVENTORY

We can deal with stress more effectively when we are aware of it. Of course, it seems obvious that we are at least partly aware of our stress already, or we wouldn't be trying to control it. However, even when we are aware that we are stressed, there is much about our stress that we don't know; consequently, taking an inventory of our stress can be an enlightening experience.

Stop for a minute and think about your life. Ask yourself some questions: What is happening to me? What conflicts am I experiencing? What pressures? What frustrations? What changes? What is it that makes me feel guilty? ashamed? depressed? afraid? anxious? tense? jealous? What do I do or feel that makes me upset with myself and down on myself? What parts of myself am I trying to hide—even from close friends? As you answer these questions, see what you can learn about yourself. You will gain a better perspective on the stress in your life—and maybe a surprising one. The exercises at the end of this unit have been developed to enable you to complete this inventory systematically.

Taking inventory is very important. We cannot develop effective strategies for dealing with our stress until we know the pattern of stress we are experiencing. Once we have an understanding of the different kinds and sources of stress in our lives, we can examine them and identify key areas and key stresses. Frequently, people find that most of the stress they experience comes from one or two sources. Once those sources have been identified, effective action can be taken. Taking inventory is not simple: it takes time, effort, and patience. The exercises for this unit, particularly Exercise 3, are the longest in this guide. My experience with those who have completed these exercises in the past indicates that the results are well worth the effort. Take your time and complete the exercises thoughtfully. You need not try to complete all of them—or even one of them—in one sitting. Taking inventory is a continuous process, and you will want to do it periodically while utilizing other methods in this guide.

Once you have completed the inventory, you will find that there are many ways to organize what you have learned about your stress. You may organize it around sources and occasions for stress: Does most of it come from your job or your family? Does most of it come from outside yourself (demands, pressures) or from within (personal expectations)? Do you find yourself stressed at certain times during the day or week? Does your stress consist of only a few disturbing emotions, like anger or jealousy? Does your stress center around external tasks and situations or around people and your interactions with them?

You will need to take some time to think about situations that are stressful for you—and to ask, "Why does this situation upset me? What is it about this that makes me anxious or guilty or angry?" Get at the reasons *behind* your stress. When you ask yourself *why* you respond as you do, don't settle for the obvious, but think carefully about the situation until you have considered it thoroughly. Get behind the obvious to the thought and wishes that are so much a part of you that you don't think about them and take so much for granted that you aren't even aware of them. Maybe, for example, you're upset with your supervisor: for some people, this shows a problem with authority; for others, it might reflect fears about one's own inadequacy. Worry over money could reflect worry over providing for one's family or an unrecognized need for absolute certainty (I must know that I will have enough money for tomorrow's needs). Getting at the reasons behind the stress is essential. You may find that most of your stress centers around a few fears, needs, or problem areas, and then you can start to deal with stress in your life more effectively.

In addition to thinking each situation through carefully, you might try talking about it. Find a friend that you trust who is willing to take time to listen to you. Ask that friend to attempt to understand what you are feeling without approving or disapproving of your reactions in any way. As she listens, whenever she is not certain about how you feel or why you feel as you do, she should question you to get further information. At this point in your stress control program, you are not seeking advice but are only talking about your stressful situations to help understand them and yourself better. This procedure will not only help you complete your inventory but will also help you feel better, since talking with a friend constitutes seeking support—a very effective method of dealing with stress (see Method 20, "Seek Support").

You can also ask your friend to role play a stressful situation with you. Imagine that you are having difficulty in working things out with your father. Ask a friend to pretend to be your father and to talk with you as your father would about the situation. Your friend should take your father's point of view and act as much as he can as your father does. Even if your friend does not know your father, you can brief him about the essentials of the problem. While role play is not a substitute for actually trying to work things out with your father, it will help you to understand your feelings and the reasons behind your reactions better.

Another interesting use of role playing consists of asking your friend to play "a part" of yourself. For example, suppose you are having a problem with procrastination that is causing you considerable distress.

Ask your friend to role play you the procrastinator. The procrastinator's task is to defend himself, tell you why procrastinating is not as bad as you think, argue with you about trying to eliminate him from your life, and otherwise represent the thoughts and feelings within you which lead you to procrastinate. I have seen this device result in considerable insight on the part of the participants. The friend who role plays with you need not be an excellent actor nor need he understand your situation fully. The interaction itself will enable you to learn about your stress.

In addition to talking it over with someone and role playing, you can gain some insight into your stressful situations when working by yourself. If you are upset with someone, for example, you might pretend that he or she is in a chair near you. Talk to that person as if she were present. Say all the things you want to say, particularly the things you are reluctant to say when the person is actually with you. Don't organize or censor your thoughts—just let them come. You may be surprised at what you learn. If there is a part of you that upsets you mentally, put yourself, or that part of yourself, in a chair and talk to it. Thus, you might speak angrily for a few moments to the "procrastinator you." If you do, you will learn more about why procrastination bothers you so much. This suggestion may seem a bit strange. We aren't used to talking to empty chairs! It will feel awkward at first. But a fuller understanding of your stress is essential, and this exercise will certainly help. So try it—if it feels silly, okay. In time, the silliness will wear off, and you will gain the benefits of the exercise.

Still another way to gain insight into the reasons behind your stress is to utilize the *awareness exercise*. This important and extremely useful exercise will not only add to your understanding of your own stress but will also help you deal with it. The best way to use the exercise is to read the directions (see the exercises at the end of this unit) and become familiar enough with them that you can do the exercises without referring to them.

Awareness and inventory, then, are accomplished by listing the sources of stress in your life, organizing that material, asking yourself why each situation results in stress, talking out some of the situations with yourself and another person, and utilizing the awareness exercise.

EXERCISES

1.   In the left-hand column below, list the major sources of stress in your life. Note the source briefly, using any terms that make sense to you. You might name specific people, indicate particular responsibilities, note certain situations, etc. In the right-hand column, list *why* that person, responsibility, situation, etc. is stressful to you. Use the awareness exercise to help you.

(Note: After completing this exercise, you may want to keep a notebook with you for a week and jot down additional sources of stress as they occur to you. You may not think of all sources of stress in one sitting.)

SOURCE OF STRESS	REASON WHY THIS IS STRESSFUL
_____	_____
_____	_____
_____	_____
_____	_____
_____	_____
_____	_____
_____	_____

2.   Stress has been defined as the experiencing of unpleasant or uncomfortable feelings. In brief, we experience stress by feeling bad. Below are listed a number of unpleasant/uncomfortable feelings. After each one list a situation or situations that evoke that particular feeling in you and indicate why you react as you do.

Anger, rage: _____

_____

_____

Anxiety, fear: _____

_____

_____

Guilt, shame, humiliation: _____

_____

_____

Frustration: _____

_____

_____

Panic: _____

_____

_____

_____

Jealousy: _____

_____

_____

Insecurity: _____

_____

_____

Hopelessness: _____

_____

_____

Helplessness: _____

_____

_____

Worry: _____

_____

_____

Upset: _____

_____

_____

Embarrassment: _____

_____

_____

_____

3. The Stressful Emotion Chart lists a variety of unpleasant/un-comfortable emotions in the left-hand column. Record in the next column to the right, under the word *Extent,* a number indicating how much, in general, you experience each emotion. Use the following rating scale:

    1 =   I *rarely* experience this emotion. (Less than once a month)

2 =   I *sometimes* (more than once a month) experience this emotion.

3 =   I *often* (once a week) experience this emotion.

4 =   I *quite frequently* (several times a week) experience this emotion.

5 =   I *almost always* (daily) experience this emotion.

When you have completed the column entitled Extent, note that the next column is entitled Self. In this column you will record the extent to which you experience each emotion in reaction to something in yourself, e.g., thoughts you have, things you do or don't do, or habits you have. Here you are recording how often you are angry at yourself, ashamed of yourself, or worried about yourself. Use the system described above for your ratings. Thus, if you are angry at yourself almost every day, you would put a 5 in the row labeled Anger, in the column headed Self. (In this part of the exercise and those that follow, there may be some emotions which won't apply. In those instances, you may record a 0 or leave the space blank.)

When you have completed the Self column, list, in the place for headings for the next several columns, those people who are important in your life and with whom you have frequent or important contact. Then, under the name of each person, put a number from 1 to 5 by each emotion (using the following system) that indicates how often your contacts with that person result in your experiencing that emotion. The system for the numbers is as follows:

1 =   I *rarely* (5% of the time) experience this emotion in my relationships with this person.

2 =   I *sometimes* (6–35% of the time) experience this emotion in my relationships with this person.

3 =   I *often* (35–70% of the time) experience this emotion in my relationships with this person.

4 =   I *quite frequently* (71–90% of the time) experience this emotion in my relationships with this person.

5 =   I *almost always* (91–100% of the time) experience this emotion in my relationships with this person.

Thus, if you are angry with your brother about 75 percent of the time you have dealings with him, you would place a 4 in the row to the right of Anger, in the column headed by the name of your brother.

When you have completed all the columns of significant people, list, in the next set of columns, situations which you encounter frequently in your life: specific situations at work (report writing, interruptions, etc.), dealing with the phone company or electric company, shopping, housework, dating, managing money—any situation which is an important part of your life. Then, using the same system as you used in describing your relationships with people, put a number under each situation indicating how much of the time being in that situation results in your experiencing each particular emotion. Thus, if you are angry every time you are interrupted at work, then you would put a 5 in the row to the right of Anger under the heading Interruptions. (You need not use the situations listed here. They are only suggestions and a means to help you list those situations which are important to you.)

In the last row, labeled Total, insert the sum of the numbers in each column. Study these totals and the chart in general to see what patterns emerge. Note where and with whom most of your stress seems to occur.

4. *Awareness exercise:* Seat yourself in a relatively comfortable chair. Take a minute or two to let yourself settle down and relax. You know your mental set when you sit at a desk and are about to engage in some serious work—and you know your mental set when you lie on the beach with the idea of doing nothing. Pretend that you are settling back for a long period of rest. This mental set is important because it enables you to let go and permit thoughts to come to you. Think of this exercise not as one in which you are going to figure anything out but as one in which you are going to sit back and let answers come to you. This *receptive attitude* is essential. As you get settled in the chair, close your eyes and keep them closed for the duration of the exercise. For a minute or two, try very hard to hear every sound around you. Strain to hear everything that is going on. Even when you are alone in a quiet place there will be some noises. Listen carefully and strain to be sure that you don't miss a single one. After a minute or so of this, change your attitude. Stop trying to hear all the sounds around you, and instead, let the sounds come to you. Don't reach out to hear them—let them come to you. Think, "If those sounds want to be heard, they will have to come to me." Sit back and let them come. Then, return to the earlier attitude of straining to hear the sounds; after a minute or so, return again to the attitude of letting the sounds come. After doing this for a few minutes, first straining to hear the sounds and then settling back and letting them come to you, you will feel the difference in these two attitudes. You will notice how more comfortable it is to let sounds come to you. When you are able to notice the difference in these two attitudes, proceed to the next step.

STRESSFUL EMOTION CHART

	Extent	Self	People													Situations									
Anger																									
Shame, Guilt																									
Fear, Anxiety																									
Depression																									
Frustration																									
Panic																									
Jealousy																									
Insecurity																									
Hopelessness																									
Helplessness																									
Worry																									
Upset																									
Embarrassment																									
Total																									

Now let yourself be aware of your body as well as the sounds around you. Let different sensations from your body make themselves known to you just as you have learned to let the sounds in the room come to you. Then, let whatever thoughts or feelings that you have within you come to you. That is, you are not going to try to think about anything at all, but you are just going to relax and *be aware* and let thoughts, feelings, and sensations come to you. We'll call this experience *being aware.*

After you have done this a few times, you will get the feel of it. You can then use this experience in two different ways. (1) Sometime when you are stressed, when you feel angry, or uneasy, or tense, sit down and just *be aware.* That is, practice the awareness exercise. Don't try to figure out why you feel as you do, but just let your thoughts and feelings come. Soon you will learn more about why you feel as you do. (2) Even when you are not currently concerned about a given situation but want to know more about it, you can use your imagination to relive the situation. With your eyes closed, remind yourself of a situation which concerns you and, instead of thinking about it or analyzing it, just imagine it happening again. Then, after working it through in your imagination for a while, just *be aware.* You will discover more about why you feel as you do.

Reactions to this exercise: _____

_____

_____

_____

_____

_____

_____

_____

_____

METHOD 2

RECOGNIZE STRESS AS PART OF LIFE

Stress is an unavoidable part of life. It's natural, inevitable, and to be expected by all of us. Unfortunately, we frequently overlook this obvious fact and mistakenly assume that everything in life should go smoothly. As a result, when difficulties do occur, we overreact and become upset or angry or anxious unnecessarily. When we learn to accept problems as natural and normal, we will respond more realistically and effectively.

Remember that this guide defines *stress* as our internal reaction to demands and events in our lives. In this unit we are emphasizing the internal component of stress. If we recognize that life inevitably brings demands and pressures (external component), then we can better manage our reaction (internal component) when those demands and pressures occur.

We cannot avoid stressful situations. Remember Murphy's law: If anything can go wrong, it will. Although the situation usually isn't that bad, it is true that we should assume, as we engage in work and personal relationships, that we will inevitably encounter difficulties and frustrations. Thus we can expect and anticipate stress. Do you own a car? Something will go wrong with it. Do you have children? They will not always do what they are told. Do you go shopping? Stores will sometimes be crowded, and merchandise will sometimes be defective. Are you employed? Your co-workers will sometimes be unreliable.

There is one easy way to increase stress in your life: ignore the last paragraph and expect everything to go your way. Strangely enough many of us do just that without realizing it. We do not anticipate difficulties. We make detailed schedules without allowing for the possibility that events may not happen as planned. We are caught by surprise when the unexpected happens.

How do we react under such circumstances? We get angry and upset and act as though life was especially unfair to us. We kick the tire that goes flat, implying that such things should never happen to us. We become angry when our boss, teacher, or family member does something we don't like, forgetting that people aren't always going to do what we want. It's easy to think, "How terrible! This shouldn't happen to me!"

Assume for a minute that you are applying for a new job. Certainly you will want everything to go smoothly. But think of what typical, normal difficulties might appear. You go to type your resume and find that you are out of paper. The bus you want to take to the office is late. When you do arrive, you find that the other applicants are ahead of you. There are questions in the interview you hadn't anticipated and you can't use the answers you had planned carefully. These things happen to everyone and can happen to you. How will you react to such difficulty? If you implicitly assume that everything will go well, you will be quite angry and upset. If you accept difficulties as natural and inevitable, you will react more calmly and be in a better position to handle it. You will also be in a better position to adopt a problem-solving approach (Method 3).

This means that we can reduce stress if we cultivate the attitude of *accepting* realities in life. *Accepting* realities means recognizing their existence without undue upset, anger, or resentment. It means taking life as it comes and responding to it as it is without demanding that it be otherwise. Acceptance allows us to stop saying, "This should not happen to me," and to say instead, "I'll take what happens and work with it. I can live with this right now."

For example, after years of giving talks to many different audiences, I've learned (as have other public speakers) that people will often misinterpret what I say. In the question and answer period after talks, they will ask questions that were clearly answered in the talk and will offer critiques of ideas which I never presented. No matter how clear I try to be, this always happens. I can be angry at people for not listening or angry at myself for not communicating clearly. I can give up trying to get my ideas across. Or I can accept the fact that communication with groups of people is usually difficult and that anytime a person addresses a group, there is a good possibility of misunderstanding and miscommunication. If I don't accept this reality, I'll be angry and upset every time! After accepting it, I can work to improve communication and feel better in the process.

There are many realities, major and minor, that we must all learn to recognize and to accept:

> *We can't have everything.*
> *Things won't always go our way.*
> *There is injustice in life.*
> *Some people will never understand us.*
> *We can't please everyone.*
> *Traffic is slow during rush hours.*

We can eliminate an enormous amount of stress in life if we also learn to accept ourselves as human beings with faults and limitations.

One of the tragedies of living is that many people never do this. Instead, they reject themselves, feel guilty about their limitations, and condemn themselves for not reaching the unrealistically high goals they have set for themselves. If you are such a person, you will gain enormous relief by recognizing your faults, accepting your limits, and learning to be on good terms with yourself.

Can you accept yourself as you are right now? Can you look at yourself and say, "I'm okay now." If you are not self-accepting, then you probably have thoughts and feelings which make you feel guilty. You may even feel guilty about being *you!* How much more stress do we experience when we fill our days with self-criticism and self-rejection? How much better our lives would be if we could only learn to see ourselves as humans who are not perfect but who are nevertheless worthy of acceptance.

The psychologist Carl Rogers tells us that we often develop *conditions of worth*. We think to ourselves, "I am worthy *if* I live up to certain standards or conditions." Some people feel worthy only if they are working very hard all the time. Others feel unworthy if they are not as loving towards others as they were told they should be. Others ask themselves to do everything perfectly before considering themselves worthy people. The number of possible conditions of worth is unlimited. Self-acceptance is rejecting conditions of worth and saying, "I can accept myself now even though I am not as good or as perfect as I'd like to be."

All of us have faults and limitations. If we look at ourselves, we'll see that there are times when we are irrational or irresponsible. Don't we all have moments of childishness or immaturity? or feelings and wishes of which we are not proud? We are human beings and to be human is to think and act and feel like humans. Humans also have their limits; there are things which we can't do no matter how hard we try. When we learn to accept our humanness, we eliminate the guilt and self-criticism that self-rejection brings.

Many people have difficulty with the idea of acceptance—particularly self-acceptance. They feel that self-accepting people are smug and self-satisfied. They fear that the self-accepting person has no values or standards and will give up trying to improve. Acceptance of reality seems to them to be a passive, apathetic approach to life—giving in to life's difficulties rather than fighting them.

An accepting person is not that way at all. Acceptance is *not* liking; acceptance is *not* agreeing; acceptance is *not* indifference; acceptance is *not* failure to act for change. We can accept the fact that life isn't always fair without liking it. We can deplore injustice, work to reduce it, and still accept that it exists. Our battle can be enthusiastic, energetic, and effective without our being angry, resentful, or emotionally upset. Rather than being indifferent or apathetic, we can accept the reality of injustice and also accept the fact that we must do something about it.

Strange though it may seem, the failure to accept often leads to less work for change. We get so caught up in our resentment and anger that we use our energy dealing with these emotions rather than with the reality that needs changing.

The same is true of self-acceptance. When we do not accept ourselves, we feel guilty and self-critical. Rarely does this prompt us to improve. We can feel guilty and self-rejecting for years and yet never change. Moreover, our attention gets turned from our real difficulties to our guilt and self-rejection. We begin to find ways to justify ourselves and explain away our guilt. In other words, our self-rejection replaces our faults as the focus of our attention. One way to get rid of our unpleasant feeling about our limitations is to pretend that these limitations don't exist. A person who is ashamed of his anger will soon learn to pretend that he isn't angry. The more we hide our thoughts and feelings, the less we will know ourselves. When we live with an image of ourselves as we'd like to be rather than as we are, we certainly aren't ready to work on correcting our faults. Thus self-acceptance is necessary for self-improvement. Rather than cause us to be smug and self-satisfied, acceptance helps us see our faults and thus puts us in a better position to do something about them.

We can have high standards and strive for improvement and still be self-accepting. We can accept ourselves as we are while still trying to be better. If we did not, then in effect, efforts at improvement would really be efforts at self-acceptance. Suppose, for example, that a young woman has the desire to be a loving person but knows that she is unkind and jealous from time to time. She can accept herself with her unkindness and jealousy and still strive to be more loving. If she does not, then she will strive to be loving more to be able to accept herself than to be loving for its own sake. Ironic, isn't it?

Sometimes, however, we must accept certain realities or parts of ourselves that we cannot change. A person of fifty years of age must accept the fact that he will never be thirty again. No matter how hard we try, there will be some people who will never accept or even understand our point of view. In such instances, the mature approach is to accept the fact that there is little or nothing we can do. Admittedly there will be times when we can't decide whether change is possible or not. At such times remember the old anonymous prayer, "God, grant me the courage to change those things I can change, the serenity to accept those things I cannot change, and the wisdom to tell one from the other."

We can learn to be more accepting by thinking about the advantages of acceptance and the problems that lack of acceptance brings. Acceptance comes also through giving up unspoken rules such as, *I must be perfect,* or *Everything must go my way,* or *People must be what I want them to be* (See Method 7, "Revise Unspoken Rules"). Giving up excessive demands that we make on ourselves (see Method 15, "Reduce Demand") will also help. Finally, the exercise at the end of this unit will guide you in other specific ways of learning to be more accepting.

EXERCISE

Make a list of realities that you must accept, i.e., realities that are very much a part of life and which you can do little or nothing about, at least for the moment. Think about each of them carefully. Why not accept them? Why say it necessarily should be different? How does it feel when you accept them? How does it feel when you refuse to accept them and fight their existence? What price do you pay for these feelings? Record your reactions below.

I recognize the following as realities that I can learn to accept:

_____

_____

_____

_____

_____

_____

_____

_____

_____

_____

_____

Reactions to thinking through the questions about acceptance:

_____

_____

_____

_____

_____

_____

_____

_____

_____

_____

_____

METHOD 3

ADOPT A PROBLEM-SOLVING APPROACH

Once we learn to recognize stress as a natural part of life, we can then adopt a problem-solving attitude toward it. We can learn to view stress as a problem to be solved rather than as an injustice inflicted on us. When we stop resenting the demands and frustrations of our lives and start accepting their reality and approaching them as problems to be solved, we can significantly decrease the stress we experience.

Think of a politician running for office. A novice candidate might naively assume that he could make his case known to the public through speeches and publications, that he would be judged on his merits, and that the public would vote rationally on the basis of all the information they received from him and other candidates. That isn't the way it happens. That politician will regularly be frustrated in his efforts to make his case before the public. If he gives a long, brilliant speech to a large audience, during which a large dog unexpectedly runs through the room upsetting everyone, the press will give more coverage to the dog than to the speech. The quotes in the press of his speech will rarely represent his ideas as he would wish. Unfair charges made by his opponents or false rumors about his past will never be adequately refuted. Long, complicated papers on his views will not be read by most of the people. On election day, his religion, hair cut, or marital problems may affect people's votes more than any rational consideration of his position on the issues and his qualifications.

Our politician friend can respond by becoming angry and resentful, complaining that politics isn't fair and that people should learn to treat him better. He can become bitter and cynical, letting the frustrations of the campaign eat away at him. Or he can do what any successful campaigner does: accept certain realities of political and public life and see the difficulties they create as problems to be solved. Thus, if the press never gives (or never seems to give) adequate coverage, the politician will prepare brief quotable statements that reporters are sure to pick up. If people won't go to political rallies, he will go to where they are and talk to them. He will see the entire campaign as the problem of getting elected in a somewhat unfair, irrational system and will do what can be done to address that problem.

Like the politician, we can view difficulties in our lives as problems to be solved. Imagine that you are the parent of a teen-ager who wants to go out on dates, participate in sports, and own a car but who refuses to do chores around the house. This very common situation usually provokes considerable stress in the parent. Can you see this as a problem needing a solution, instead of getting angry at the teen-ager and wishing he or she were different? Can you ask yourself how you might work with or reason with her or him so as to improve the situation? If you begin thinking this way, then the anger and resentment will subside and you will approach the problem in an entirely different frame of mind. You can begin thinking this way by completing the exercise at the end of this unit. With practice you can learn to approach all stressful situations with an active problem-solving approach.

When we take a problem-solving approach to our stressful situations, we also move from just thinking about problems to doing something about them. Often we increase our stress by worrying about and fretting over difficulties rather than taking steps to deal with them. Anytime you are experiencing stress, ask yourself, "Is there anything I can do to deal with this situation? What specific action can I take to make things better?" Formulate a concrete plan of action to deal with the situation. Such a plan gives us a sense of control (see Method 16, "Assume Control") and gets us actively involved in solving our problems.

Action often takes time and effort and sometimes it seems easier to let time pass without doing anything, except thinking, "If only things were different, how much better I would feel." Someone once said that life is what happens to you when you are busy making other plans! Instead of fretting, complaining, and worrying, try to do something! It can make a difference in how you feel about the situation. If you're upset with a teen-ager, talk with him. If a neighbor borrows things and doesn't return them, go and ask for them back. If you're worried about retirement, go to a preretirement-planning workshop. Each small concrete action you take helps you move from a passive to an active problem-solving approach. Action also helps us grow (see Method 4, "Use Stress for Growth"), and attacking our difficulties frequently leads to learning new skills and competencies (see Method 11, "Develop Competencies").

EXERCISE

Select three or more situations that are stressful for you. Seat yourself comfortably in a chair, close your eyes, and imagine yourself in one of these situations. Fantasize about that situation for a few minutes, experiencing the situation as vividly as you can. Focus for a while on how you feel about the situation. Dwell on your anger, anxiety, or frustration. Think about how much you dislike the situation and wish it were not occurring. Then switch your focus: begin thinking about the situation itself as a problem to be solved. Let your thoughts move from your own reactions and feelings to questions which will help you begin to work on the problem: What is the cause of the difficulty? What is there in me or in the demand that needs changing? What might I learn to accept? What resources can I use in handling this situation? What are the various possible approaches to solving this problem and the advantages and disadvantages of each? Repeat this procedure with each of the situations you have selected. Note your reactions to the two ways of thinking and record them below.

Reactions to this exercise:

_____

_____

_____

_____

_____

_____

_____

_____

_____

_____

METHOD 4

USE STRESS FOR GROWTH

We think of stress as bad for us—and it is. In this guide stress is discussed in its negative sense. However, even unwelcome stress can be used for good. An effective way to manage stress, therefore, is to use stressful situations as opportunities for growth.

The Chinese symbol for crisis has two characters: one means danger; the other means opportunity. That is what a crisis is: a situation that presents danger but also offers an opportunity. Whether a difficult situation turns out to be more of a danger or more of an opportunity depends very much on us.

Our initial reaction to stress is often nonproductive. When we find ourselves short of funds at the end of the month, we worry or get angry. When we find ourselves faced with a task that seems impossible for us, we sometimes give up. Frequently we give in to excessive demands placed on us by others rather than stand up for our rights. A reaction of frustration and anger to stressful situations not only makes us feel bad but also blinds us to the fact that stress can help us grow. Adopting a problem-solving approach (see Method 3) helps us develop new skills and gain new insights into ourselves. Thus, we can learn to see stressful situations as opportunities for growth.

When I was in the sixth grade, our teacher told several of us that we had to memorize poetry and recite it in the school assembly. She gave me a poem with three long verses. I asked which verse she wanted me to learn. To my horror, she wanted all three. I couldn't believe it! I couldn't memorize that much and then stand up in front of the entire school and recite it. But children did not say no to this teacher; so I did it. I fretted and worried, but I did it. When it was over I learned something about myself: I could memorize three long verses and recite them to the entire school.

Many times in my life I developed skills and stretched my capabilities because I had to face a stressful situation. Now I'm grateful for the times when I was given a job that seemed beyond my capabilities and forced me to grow into it. All of us can use a challenging situation as an opportunity to grow. When we feel the stress of a difficult situation, we can lessen it by saying to ourselves, "This is an opportunity to grow."

For example, students often complain to me about having a difficult

26

roommate. That is certainly a bad situation. In addition to all the other things I suggest to help the student, I also say, "Look, you will have to learn to live with all types of people during your lifetime. Someday you may have a teacher or supervisor who is unreasonable or difficult. Thus, while no one would want you to have a difficult roommate, now that you're in this situation, realize that you have the opportunity to learn how to live with an unreasonable person. That skill will be of great benefit to you all your life."

Of course, not everyone likes that type of advice. But it is true that crises can be used for growth. Take the man who had the unpleasant task of firing a subordinate. The supervisor was quiet, meek, and had a very thin skin. He could not imagine himself telling a subordinate that his work was unsatisfactory and he would have to leave. The more he thought about it, the more worried he became, and the worse he felt. But then he changed his attitude. He reasoned, "I must learn to handle this type of situation. I have to develop thicker skin if I'm going to continue as a supervisor. I can use this unpleasant task as an opportunity to grow." His change in attitude did not make his problem go away, but it did help him deal with it rather than avoiding it, and made the entire process much less uncomfortable.

When we continually run out of money at the end of the month, we can grow by learning how to manage a budget. Growth also comes when we learn to organize our time and set priorities when we have too much work and not enough time in which to do it (see Method 15A, "Establish Priorities"). If we can learn how to stand up for our rights and refuse unreasonable demands, we grow considerably in our ability to relate to other people.

Take any stressful situation and see if you can find within it an opportunity to grow. Then welcome that opportunity. This does not mean liking the stressful situation; instead, it means taking a bad situation and using it for a good purpose. The exercises at the end of this unit will help you think about how some difficulties in the past have helped you grow and how those you face now can be used for growth.

EXERCISES

1. Select three or more situations that were stressful for you in the past. Describe each one in a few sentences. For each one, ask yourself, "What did I learn from that situation? What did I learn about myself? What did I learn about others and the world? What skills did I gain or what did I learn to do? How did I change as a result of this situation?" Your answers to these questions indicate how you grew in each situation.

Situation 1:_____

_____

_____

How I grew:_____

_____

_____

Situation 2:_____

_____

_____

How I grew:_____

_____

_____

Situation 3:_____

_____

_____

How I grew:_____

_____

_____

2. Select three or more situations that are currently stressful for you. Describe each one in a few sentences. Ask yourself the questions listed in Exercise 1 to determine how you can use each situation for growth.

Situation 1:_____

_____

_____

How I can grow:_____

_____

_____

Situation 2:_____

_____

_____

How I can grow:_____

_____

_____

Situation 3:_____

_____

_____

How I can grow:_____

_____

_____

PART II

WORKING ON YOURSELF

Now that you've taken an inventory of your current stress and have begun to see stress differently by recognizing it as a part of life, adopting a problem-solving approach, and using stress for growth, you are ready to look at some of the more specific steps you can take to reduce your stress reactions. Remember that stress consists of an inner reaction to events and circumstances in our lives. Thus we can reduce stress by working on our inner reactions and on external events. This part of the guide focuses on working on yourself, i.e., doing what you can to alter your inner reaction to stressful situations. Often we can do nothing about external events, but we can always work on ourselves. Learning to do this even before we work on the task results in considerable reduction of the stress we experience.

METHOD 5

TAKE CARE OF YOURSELF

Our state of mind and the condition of our body continually interact with each other. People who experience considerable stress, are in poor mental health, or are likely to worry and fret more than others have an increased risk of physical illness. Experts have studied the relationship between physical illness and emotional well-being extensively, and while there are many unanswered questions in this complicated and fascinating subject, there is no doubt that our emotional well-being does affect our general physical health. Increasingly the literature points to the fact that excessive experience with stress leads to illness and disease. In fact, many experts feel that there is a mental or emotional component in most physical illness.

People frequently overlook the fact that the opposite is true as well, namely, that our physical condition affects our mental state. When we are tired and run-down, we are more prone to overreact to stressful situations than when we are well rested. If a person fails to get enough sleep and exercise, she or he will become angry or upset more easily than otherwise. When we work without taking time to relax and let go for a while, tensions can build, and we then explode at some insignificant event. Recent studies suggest that our eating and drinking habits play a larger role in how we feel about ourselves and relate to others than most of us realize. Have you seen the television ads that portray the coffee drinker as irritable and easily upset? There is truth in those ads. Data on the effects of caffeine implicate that substance in a variety of unpleasant personal reactions.

You are aware of the fact that there are times when you are more easily irritated and angered. Today's traffic jam nearly put you into a rage, while yesterday's presented no problem at all. You became very angry when you felt your wife wasn't listening to you at home, but understood her preoccupation with her interests at another time. There are many reasons why we respond differently in different situations and at different times, and our physical condition is one of the most important of them. The more we push ourselves, sleep erratically, eat improperly, and exercise irregularly, the more we will find ourselves tense, irritable, and unreasonable, and the more we will overreact to stressful situations.

What can we do about this? We can learn to take care of ourselves. If we get into the habit of looking after our health, of letting go, of taking it easy once in a while, and of slowing down, we can reduce our stress considerably.

Unfortunately, people who most need to learn to take care of themselves are most apt to resist doing so. People who complain that they are pressured, hassled, and overworked also feel that they don't have the time to stop and relax. The woman who rushes frantically from activity to activity to meet the demands of her career and her family understandably argues, "I have no more time." And looking after yourself does take time. The grade-conscious college student, anxious about his abilities, feels that every minute spent relaxing is lost to studying. The person heavily involved in community projects who already feels overworked and over-burdened exclaims, "What? You want me to take time out to relax?" Often I have given a relaxation tape to people complaining of always feeling tense and tired, only to have them tell me months later that they didn't have time to play the tape!

You may sincerely believe that you do not have the time to take care of yourself, but that belief must be challenged. We don't *find* time for this purpose—we *take* time. We must decide that slowing down and letting go are important. Can you make it a priority for yourself? (See Method 15A "Establish Priorities"). If you do, then you will make the time to do those things that are required.

You might find it easier to establish taking care of yourself as a priority if you realize that in the long run, it saves you time rather than costs you time. When we have been frantically busy for a long period of time, we tire and begin to lose our efficiency. We think less clearly, we take longer to do our work, and then we worry about our reduced effectiveness and respond by working even harder and even less efficiently. A person who is tired and run-down—and worried about work—can do much less in an hour than a person who's refreshed and rested. If you take the time to let go and become refreshed, when you return to your activities you will more than make up for "lost" time.

Overwork also affects the way we think about ourselves and relate to others. As noted earlier, when tired and frustrated, we become short-tempered, irritable, hard to get along with—you know the rest. When something goes wrong, it upsets us more than usual, and that only makes the situation worse. People who say they don't have the time to relax are kidding themselves if they believe that they can keep up a hectic pace without paying the price.

There is one other reason for deciding to take care of yourself. You are reading this guide so that you might respond more constructively to stress in your life. Your ability to make use of the methods discussed here depends in part on your physical condition. If you are tired and exhausted when you pick up this guide, you will find it much more difficult to implement the methods for stress management offered here. Efforts to control our stress require energy in the same way that all our activities do. Give yourself a chance: take care of yourself.

5A—GET ADEQUATE REST

If we are to prevent ourselves from being overly tired and run-down, we need to get adequate sleep and rest. We can lose sleep for short periods without suffering noticeable harm, but adequate sleep is essential in the long run for physical and mental health. Don't overlook your need for adequate rest, too. Take a few minutes during each day to rest. When working on long projects, take a short break every hour or two. The student who studies for fifty minutes and then rests for ten will study longer and learn more than one who crams for four hours straight. So too with the executive writing a report. Work that requires heavy concentration (like memorizing) needs more frequent breaks; other work, such as planning sessions that involve interaction with other people, might need less frequent breaks, although a short break usually perks up the participants.

5B—SLOW DOWN

When you notice yourself rushing and getting tense, try to slow down deliberately. Take any activity and do it slowly and carefully. You might try taking twice the time to get washed and dressed in the morning. Or, when walking, walk slowly. All of us would benefit if we would take our time at meals, eating in a relaxed and easy manner. Instead we take our problems with us to our meals, hold meetings at lunch, pay no attention to what we are eating, and leave the table as tired as we began. Select some regular activity and decide to engage in that activity slowly and deliberately each day.

5C—UTILIZE DEEP, QUIET BREATHING

One simple way to let go is to sit down, or lie down, close your eyes, and breath deeply and quietly for a few minutes. Actually, for this exercise, five minutes is a long time. You can consciously take slow, deep, breaths. You can try holding your breath; take a deep breath, hold it for a count of five, and then let it out. Then, keep increasing the count until you are holding your breath for longer periods of time. Another variation is to establish a rhythm by counting as you inhale to a count of five, hold your breath for a count of five, and then exhale to a count of five. There is no magic to the number five—use any count which is comfortable for you. You will be amazed at how good you will feel after only a few minutes of this, and you can do this even in the middle of a busy day.

5D—RELAX

While many methods of taking care of ourselves qualify as relaxation, some are designed specifically to produce a quiet state of deep relaxation. People are often advised to relax and, strange though it may seem, they don't know how to do it. Relaxation is a skill. You can learn to relax deeply and you will find the state of relaxation you attain comfortable and wonderful. Unfortunately, methods of relaxation are difficult to teach on the printed page: personal instruction or an audio cassette offer far superior ways of learning. You will want to take advantage of at least one of the methods listed below.

Relaxation Tape

A method of deep relaxation is taught on the tape *Introduction to Deep Relaxation*, published by Social Science Research Associates (60 Glenwild Road, Madison, NJ 07940).[1] This tape provides inexpensive and easy instruction and uses a method which results in a very deep state of relaxation. After using the tape, you will be able to put yourself into a state of deep relaxation in three minutes or less.

Meditation

The cheapest and best method I know of learning meditation at home is produced by Dr. Pat Carrington and is called *Clinically Standardized Meditation*.[2] Watch your local newspaper for other possibilities.

Biofeedback

Biofeedback is an effective method for learning to relax but has some disadvantages as well. Biofeedback usually teaches you to relax one

---

[1]You can order a tape directly from Social Science Research. Enclose $7.00 with your order (plus 5% sales tax if you are a New Jersey resident).
[2]For details, write to Pace Educational Systems, Inc., P.O. Box 113, Kendall Park, NJ 08824.

muscle or part of your body at a time, and researchers disagree on whether this generalizes to the rest of your body. Biofeedback can also be more expensive than other forms of relaxation. You will probably do as well with the relaxation tape or meditation instruction, but you should be aware of biofeedback for particularly difficult situations. Physicians frequently use biofeedback in the treatment of hypertension.

Yoga

Many people find yoga exercises very relaxing. Yoga is a form of exercise which is done so slowly and easily that it induces relaxation. If you are interested in taking some yoga lessons, check your local "Y," newspaper, or telephone book. Most communities have several groups which offer lessons at low cost.

There are two sources of written instruction which will be helpful if you cannot obtain personal recorded instruction. Herbert Benson's book, *The Relaxation Response*,[1] offers an alternative to standard meditation, and *Behavior Therapy Techniques*[2] by Wolpe and Lazarus has an appendix giving instruction for progressive relaxation which involves tightening and relaxing the various muscles in the body.

5E—DEVELOP PRESENT AWARENESS

You will understand the idea of present awareness better if you will now put this guide down, take a short walk around the room, and then come back to this page. . . . Did you do it? What went through your mind as you walked around? Perhaps you were thinking, "I wonder what this is all about? This is silly. This is fun." Or maybe your mind turned to other things and you found yourself thinking about something you must do tomorrow or something that happened to you in the past. The point is that most of the time there is a constant chatter going on in our heads. We are always thinking about something—talking to ourselves. Much of the time we are either thinking about (and worrying about) the future or reminding ourselves (and often regretting) the past. While we are letting our thoughts wander to the past or the future, we are not fully in the present. You know how you can take a long drive and not even notice where you are going. At other times we eat a meal but never even pay much attention to the food. This tendency to be somewhere other than the present creates difficulty for us in two ways:

[1]Benson, H. *The Relaxation Response.* New York: Avon, 1975.
[2]Wople, J. and Lazarus, A. *Behavior Therapy Techniques.* New York: Pergamon Press, 1966.

1. This constant inner chatter takes energy and contributes to our stress.
2. The problems of the future and the past interfere with our enjoyment of the present.

Suppose that you could take a walk around the room and be totally in the present—not thinking about the past, future, or anything at all but just experiencing all that was in the room. That would be a great experience! You would be very relaxed because nothing at all would be bothering you; since you were just experiencing the present, no problem or difficulty would be on your mind. Even if you faced a stressful situation tomorrow, if you developed this present awareness, you would not fret over it today. The mistakes of the past cannot bother me if I am totally in today's present.

Being totally in the present all the time is not possible for us, nor is it advisable. But developing the ability to be more in the present than we usually are can be an effective means of relaxing and renewing ourselves.

How can you increase your present awareness? There is a simple way to do this, and you have learned most of it already. In the section on taking inventory (Method 1), you were introduced to the *awareness exercise*. If you have not already done so, read those directions and practice that exercise until you are quite familiar with it. When using the awareness exercise to take inventory, you were seated with your eyes closed. You can also practice awareness with your eyes open and while you are engaging in some daily activity. To begin, select some routine activity which you do alone, e.g., taking a shower. As you shower, try to be as aware as you can of yourself, your surroundings, the water falling on you, and all other present sensations. Each time your mind wanders and you begin to think about what you must do later in the day or begin to worry about some problem, let those thoughts go and return to just being aware of yourself in the present. Don't strain to be aware; let all sensations come to you. You might also try this present awareness as you eat your breakfast, drive to work, or engage in some other routine activity. Another very good time is one brief period spent lying in bed right after waking up or just before going to sleep. Gradually you will expand the time when your mind is not cluttered with endless chatter, and you will find yourself becoming more relaxed and less stressed.

Remember that present awareness is easy so long as you don't push it too far. That is, there is no way in which we can be totally in the present without our minds wandering to some extent. Expect that to happen and don't let it upset you. Just gently turn your attention to the present whenever you find that this happens—which will be every few seconds. Let this be an easy exercise: if you set out to free your mind of all thoughts, you will fail and then be angry with yourself and increase your stress. If, on the other hand, you set out to increase your present awareness even a little, you will succeed and enjoy the success. This is a powerful and effective exercise; it's worth practicing. Since you are doing it while engaging in some routine activity, it takes no extra time at all.

5F—DEVELOP A DAILY ROUTINE

An effective means of slowing down and letting go is to develop a routine of some sort which takes about one-half hour and which we can engage in daily. Most people find that they can work a routine into their lives on a regular basis even if they can't do it every day. For example, one person might end each day by taking a shower and listening to music for twenty minutes or so. Another might read the newspaper after returning from work and before dinner. Another might have a friend that could be called each day for a chat. The possibilities are limitless, but the idea is always the same: develop some reasonably quiet, enjoyable routine which takes about a half hour and try to engage in that routine at the same time each day.

5G—WATCH YOUR PHYSICAL HEALTH

The first six ways to take care of yourself (adequate rest; slowing down; deep, quiet breathing; relaxation; present awareness; daily routine) are all ways of letting go. They are ways of relaxing, taking it easy, and slowing your pace for a few minutes. The last way of taking care of your self is to watch your physical health. This unit opened with a discussion of the importance of good physical health in any stress control program. Let's review the main points of that discussion.

Considerable exciting research is being conducted continually on the intricate relationships of mind and body. Clearly, you will experience less stress if you maintain good physical health. On a very simple level, we realize that the more tired we are, the greater our problems feel, and the less energy we have to combat them. On a more complicated level, there is a great deal of research about the relationships between body chemistry (and hence diet) and our thoughts and feelings. While many questions in this area remain unanswered, we know enough to realize that the maintenance of good physical health is important in managing stress.

It is not the intent of this guide to offer a program for physical health—you will need to consult other sources for that. Now, however, you can decide to make physical health a priority and to do some thinking about the state of your health. Take a minute to ask yourself if you have been paying attention to your health. Do you engage in regular, vigorous physical exercise? Do you eat properly: three meals a day with proper nutrition? Do you get sufficient sleep and rest? College students in particular are apt to get extremely run-down by staying up until all hours of the night (and morning), skipping meals, and working for such long periods of time that they are exhausted to the point of collapse. Pressured business executives and women who both work and manage households often do the same thing. We cannot cheat on our health and get away with it for long.

If you realize that you are not taking proper care of your body, decide now that physical health must be a priority for you. Check appropriate sources on exercise, diet, and nutrition and, of course, see your physican before starting any new exercise program. If you are interested, call the nearest holistic health association. These associations have devised questionnaires that can help you decide how healthy your living habits are. Other sources of help include television programs, YM- and YWCAs, and adult education programs—all of which offer programs on exercise and nutrition. Also, your local library and bookstore have books in this area which can help you develop a plan for good physical health.

EXERCISE

Review your daily routine and determine if you are letting go as frequently as you might. In particular, see how much you use these methods for letting go: rest; slowing down; short walks; play; deep, quiet breathing; daily routine; relaxation. Record below how you can work these methods into your routine so that you can make better use of them. Then resolve to make use of these methods as soon as you can.

Rest:_____

_____

_____

_____

Slowing down:_____

_____

_____

_____

Deep, quiet breathing:_____

_____

_____

_____

Daily routine:_____

_____

_____

_____

Relaxation:_____

_____

_____

_____

Present awareness:_____

_____

_____

_____

METHOD 6

GET AWAY FROM IT ALL

Have you ever had the experience of returning home from a vacation, looking around, and finding that while your home was familiar, it also appeared new and fresh? Have you ever worked very hard to find a solution to a problem without success, only to discover a useful and seemingly obvious answer after you went for a walk? Perhaps you have taken a weekend trip and found that when you returned from this brief vacation, you were refreshed, rested, and ready to tackle your work with renewed energy and vigor. Each of these examples illustrates the value of getting away from it all—of setting our work and cares aside for a while and becoming involved in some other activity.

Frequently we have work to do or problems to solve that we cannot change in any significant way. At such times, the suggestions given in Part III of this guide are not applicable. The tasks that we face are ours, and we must complete them. After all, stressful situations arise in our relations with employers, co-workers, and family members that just don't go away. However, we can always take time to get away from it all for a while. No matter how difficult a situation may be for us, time spent away will refresh us and enable us to see it in a new light.

The last unit discussed ways that you can take better care of yourself, and this unit discusses getting away from it all for a while. These two approaches are similar in many respects. Relaxing, for example, while primarily aimed at taking care of ourselves, also takes us away from our stressful situations for a brief period. Getting away for a while by taking a walk is also relaxing. However, the emphasis in this unit is on activities that physically take us away from stressful situations and direct our attention to other activities. As a result, while these two groups of stress control methods are similar, I have put them into two separate categories. The first, Method 5, involves working on yourself, and the second, Method 6 discussed in this unit, directs your attention away from yourself and your stressful situations.

6A—CHANGE YOUR ENVIRONMENT

One way to "get away from it all" is to get away, literally. While taking a break from work helps, physically leaving the surroundings which are associated with our day-to-day concerns is essential. A person who has a week's vacation and who spends it at home is not experiencing a radical change in environment and will thus get less than the maximum rest from the vacation. At least once a year try to get away to a totally different environment for a week. Several times during the year, see if you can spend a weekend or even a day visiting a new place. We can also provide for a change in environment by having a quiet place to go: a walk in the park, a few minutes in a chapel, or time spent relaxing in a special room set aside for nothing but relaxation or meditation.

6B—GIVE YOURSELF INTRINSICALLY REWARDING EXPERIENCES

Everyone has some things that they enjoy so much that doing them absorbs their attention and in effect takes them away from their concerns for a while. An intrinsically rewarding experience is one which we enjoy for its own sake. It is one that we do, not do out of a sense of duty or because we have to, but because doing it feels good. For me, listening to music, going out to dinner, or playing a game with a child are such activities. Each of us can cite some experiences and activities that are especially enjoyable and absorbing. People usually think of a hobby in this context and a hobby is certainly intrinsically rewarding, but we need not confine ourselves to activities as structured as that. Often much less involved activities such as phoning a friend, reading a newspaper, or going to a movie are intrinsically rewarding. Remind yourself of things that you enjoy doing and that you do because you want to, not because you have to or feel you ought to. Allow yourself to do those things regularly, particularly at times when you feel tense, overworked, and stressed.

6C—PLAY

Frequently people become so involved in the serious business of living that they never play. They worry about their work; they worry about how they relate to other people; they even turn making love into work requiring hours of serious reading and serious discussion. Work is fine, but so is play. Take the time once in a while to play, whether it be actually playing a game or just taking the time to have fun. (Actually, it's all too easy to make a game into work by playing it with dead seriousness). What can you do just for fun? Throw a snowball? Jump in the leaves? Go to a movie? Make your own choice. Remember that part of play is laughter. How often do you laugh? Laughter is a great antidote to stress. Seek out and take advantage of opportunities for play and laughter.

6D—DEVELOP EXTERNAL INTERESTS

Sometimes when we are stressed, we worry so much about ourselves that we make ourselves worse. This vicious cycle feeds on itself: we are stressed; so we worry about ourselves; the worry about ourselves makes us more stressed; this greater stress produces more worry, which in turn produces more stress; and so on. It's easy to become overly preoccupied with oneself. We can break this cycle by doing something that gets our minds off ourselves and our worries and on to something external—hence, external interests. When we are involved in these interests, we let go of our concerns about ourselves. Any activity which takes our minds off ourselves and our worries qualifies. Play and intrinsically rewarding experiences will help. Another great help is to decide to do something for someone else. Collecting money for a charity, visiting a sick or lonely person, volunteering for a worthwhile cause—all of these activities can help us as much as the other person. Equally important, we should develop friendships with a variety of people, including some not associated with our work. If our social life involves only people with whom we work, we'll talk about work when out for fun, and soon our work dominates all our lives. Be with people and do things which get your mind off yourself, off your work, and off your problems.

6E—EXERCISE REGULARLY

Regular physical exercise constitutes an excellent way of getting our minds off our stressful situations and problems. As we engage in exercise, we become more and more aware of our bodies and less and less aware of the stresses of the day. Vigorous exercise can be particularly effective in absorbing our attention.

Exercise is easy and almost always possible no matter where we are or how little time we have to spare. We can work regular exercise into our routine so that it is always a part of our daily life. We can exercise alone or with others. Exercise need not cost us anything. Clearly, exercise is a useful, flexible method for controlling stress.

Those who exercise regularly have an extra advantage. Physical exercise is not only a way of getting away from it all, it is also a way of taking care of ourselves by contributing to our physical health (Method 5G). Nevertheless, many people resist the suggestion to exercise regularly. They think of exercise as resulting in exhaustion and fatigue. They suspect that it will take too much time and effort. We all know joggers who take a very long time running considerable distances each day and conclude that we must make an equal commitment to our exercise program. Some people associate exercise with workouts in a gym and worry about the costs involved. To others, exercise suggests a formal program, with classes, instruction, and fees.

Exercise can be any or all of the above, but it need not have any of these disadvantages (for those who consider time, effort, and expense disadvantageous). Exercise can be fun and rewarding. It need not take a long time nor require a great deal of effort—although if we minimize effort too much, we lose a great deal of the potential benefit. We can exercise informally, in our own homes, and without cost.

Often when I am working at my desk for long periods of time, I take a few minutes to stand up and stretch, leisurely and thoroughly. Using some techniques learned in yoga, I spend five minutes stretching various parts of my body, focusing on the physical sensations produced by this quick, easy, mild form of exercise. As a matter of fact, five minutes is a fairly long time for stretching. What could be easier than that?

Another easy exercise is taking a walk. In a slow leisurely walk, we can take the time to notice our environment, and thus turn our attention away from our stress. A brisk walk, with arms swinging, provides an excellent break from our work.

I mention these forms of exercise to point out that you can introduce exercise into your life without spending a great deal of time and effort. This observation is important since so many people resist the thought of exercise. After you have done such things as stretching or taking short walks, then you may be ready to go on to other exercises which ask more of you. Tennis, handball, bicycle riding, bowling, boating, swimming— each of these gives the opportunity to be physically active. Experts agree that swimming is one of the best exercises of all.

If you wish, you can be more formal about your exercising: jogging; workouts in a gym; aerobic dancing; isometrics. The growing popularity of these activities indicates that many people do find them helpful.

The choice is yours. Try something simple like stretching or take up a more complete exercise program. If you do not engage in much exercise at present, avoid the mistake of trying too much too soon. Frequently a well-intentioned individual who has not exercised regularly decides to undertake a full exercise program. He or she signs up for a physical fitness program at the local Y, gets a tennis partner, and starts to jog four miles each day. Such efforts as these not only endanger the individual's health, they quickly lead to exhaustion, leaving the person with the thought, "I knew I didn't like physical exercise. Why engage in it if it makes me feel this way?" Start slowly and work up to a more complete program.

As is the case in watching your physical health, make use of re-sources as you plan an exercise program. Check with your physician. Consult your library or bookstore. Visit your YM- or YWCA. Check with your adult education program. There is a great deal of help around, and it makes sense to use it. You can begin planning your exercise program, as well as other methods of getting away from it all, by completing the exercises for this unit.

EXERCISES

1.   Make a list of some of your intrinsically rewarding experiences, i.e., things which you enjoy doing very much. Put an asterisk (*) by those which you have not done recently. Put a date by which you now promise yourself you will take the time to enjoy that experience.

EXPERIENCE   DATE

_____   _____

_____   _____

_____   _____

_____   _____

_____   _____

_____   _____

_____   _____

_____   _____

_____   _____

2.   Make a list of activities you might become involved in which qualify as external interests and another list of ways in which you can change your environment (both for short periods of time and for longer periods of time). Then take the earliest opportunity to develop those external interests and to make those changes in your environment. In the plan for action, record how you can do this.

EXTERNAL INTERESTS   CHANGE IN ENVIRONMENT

_____   _____

_____   _____

_____   _____

_____   _____

Plan for action:_____

_____

_____

_____

_____

3. In the spaces provided below, make a list of types of exercises and play which are interesting and appropriate for you. If, for example, you enjoy tennis, list it; if you know you would never consider jogging, don't list it. Allow yourself to list activities which you have not participated in but are reasonably sure you would enjoy. Then, indicate how frequently in the past year you have engaged in each of these activities. Use the following rating scale to indicate frequency of activity: 1 = never; 2 = sometimes; 3 = infrequently; 4 = often; 5 = regularly.

ACTIVITY (EXERCISE OR PLAY)	FREQUENCY OF ACTIVITY				
_____	1	2	3	4	5
_____	1	2	3	4	5
_____	1	2	3	4	5
_____	1	2	3	4	5
_____	1	2	3	4	5
_____	1	2	3	4	5
_____	1	2	3	4	5
_____	1	2	3	4	5
_____	1	2	3	4	5
_____	1	2	3	4	5

Look over your list and your ratings. Are you satisfied that there is enough exercise and play in your life? If not, in the space below write out your plan for increasing these activities. Be as realistic as possible.

Plan for action:_____

_____

_____

_____

_____

METHOD 7

REVISE UNSPOKEN RULES

Have you ever thought about how many rules we obey every day? Almost every minute of every day of our lives is bound up by rules, customs, and mores. Sometimes we are aware of the rules that we are obeying. The man who puts on a coat and tie to go to a fine restaurant knows that he is obeying the rule about dress. The job seeker knows about the rule that one should not be late for appointments with a prospective employer. Most of us know and respect the rule not to break promises made to children, to laugh (or at least try to) when a friend tells a joke, or to avoid interrupting someone when he is talking.

On the other hand, there are other rules that we aren't so aware of: rules that we take so for granted that they don't seem like rules at all, but seem to outline the right or only way to behave. Until we stop and think about it, eating three meals a day seems like the natural and only way to obtain nourishment. In fact, this is a custom not adhered to in many parts of the world. Anyone who has studied life in different cultures around the world knows that many ideas that we accept as representing reality are just our way of doing things—our rules. Many of these other rules are so unnoticed that they are rarely spoken aloud: they are the unspoken rules: ideas we live by without questioning them. Some of these unspoken rules are shared by most everyone in our society, but others may be unique to a particular person.

These unspoken rules are powerful influences in our lives and trying to live up to them is a major cause of stress. The disappointment, frustration, anger, anxiety, and guilt that result from violating these unspoken rules constitute a large percent of the stress most people experience. Becoming aware of these unspoken rules, challenging them, and revising them is an effective way of managing stress in our lives. Experts in human behavior have long understood the importance of these unspoken rules, and some, e.g., Albert Ellis and Aaron Beck, have written extensively about them. The ideas in this unit are based on their excellent work.

What are some unspoken rules? Take a person who is always afraid to speak up when talking with other people. This person never offers an opinion different from a friend's. When asked to do a favor, he can never say no. Think of the stress resulting from this behavior. Such a person is living according to a number of unspoken rules, such as *I must never get anyone angry at me, or I must please everyone, or I must never think of my own needs—only the other person's.* If I live according to the rule, *I must never get anyone angry at me,* a lot of my behavior is influenced by that rule, and I pay a price for that. While I am busy spending my time doing what pleases others and avoiding what might anger them, I am neglecting my own needs and wishes, and that greatly increases my stress. Here are other common unspoken rules:

> *I must never make a mistake.*
> *I must never fail.*
> *I must never look foolish.*
> *I must work very hard at all times.*
> *I must never get angry.*
> *I must always play it safe.*

We also have a series of unspoken rules for other people: our expectations about how other people should behave toward us:

> *People should never disappoint me.*
> *People should do what I ask.*
> *People should be reasonable toward me.*
> *People should not ask me to do what I don't want to do.*

Usually, the rules for ourselves consist of "musts"—I must do this, I must be that. The rules for others consist of "shoulds"—he should to this, she should do that.

We feel bad when these rules are broken. When we break rules we have set for ourselves, we usually feel either angry or guilty. Instead of, or besides, guilt, we often experience shame, anxiety, or embarrassment. Anger is the most common response when other people break rules that we set up for them. We are angry at them and say, "They shouldn't do that; they shouldn't be that way."

Think of situations where you have been angry or guilty, or experienced some other stressful response. See if you can examine the unspoken thought process which led to that feeling. It's probably something like this:

> I made a mistake yesterday. That's terrible. *I must never make a mistake.* If I make a mistake, that means that I am stupid or foolish. Maybe it means I'm weak. Other people will think less of me. *Other people should always think the best of me. Other people should never know my weaknesses.* This is terrible; I can't stand it.

After thinking this way, we begin to disparage ourselves. Although we don't always verbalize it, we think of ourselves as unworthy people, terrible offenders, or worse, and we suffer anger, guilt, or shame.

Take the example of someone who promises to take a trip with you and backs out late in the planning. You say to yourself:

> He is a terrible person. ***People should never disappoint me.*** He made a promise, and so he should keep it—he has no right to change his mind. He's wrong and should never do this. ***People should always keep their promises to me.***

Again, although we might not verbalize it, we would be thinking that our friend was a bad or terrible person for not being what we thought she should be. If you think of times when you have been angry at other people, you will find that it was usually because they broke one of your unspoken rules by not doing or being what you thought they should.

Anxiety is another stressful emotion that results from the unspoken rules we have about ourselves and others. Think of a situation that makes you anxious. Why are you so anxious? When you think about it, you will probably discover some unspoken rule that you so firmly believe must never be broken that the very prospect of not living up to it threatens you. You are thinking, ***I must never do this,*** or ***This should never happen to me.*** You are thinking that you couldn't stand it if this rule were broken or this need were not met. The person who is anxious because he must speak before a group of strangers has a number of unspoken rules:

> *I must not make a public mistake.*
> *People must think well of me.*
> *I must not let people know of my worry or concern.*
> *I must never appear to be inadequate in front of others.*

Behind most anxiety is some unspoken rule, or collection of rules, that makes us feel as we do.

Rules help us live efficiently and effectively. There isn't much chance that we could ever do without them. Certain rules, however, get us into difficulty all the time, and these need to be revised. Usually these are the *musts* and the *shoulds*. When we think that something *must* be, or *should* be, or *has to be*, we get very upset when reality doesn't fit our demands. A *rule* is a demand—a demand that we and other people be, act, and think in ways that *we* want.

People who suffer most from stress are not necessarily those who have many external demands placed upon them, but people who place many demands on themselves and others through unspoken rules. These internal demands can be the hardest to bear. Thus, an executive who must make all the decisions, must always be in control, and never delegates responsibility is under much more stress than another executive with equal responsibility but different unspoken rules. The woman who says, "I must always succeed; I must never make a serious mistake; people should always see that I am in command," invites stress—and usually finds that invitation accepted.

Some of the difficulty stems from the type of thinking that accompanies these rules. Unspoken rules convert hopes and preferences to needs. We think in "all-or-none" terms. We tend to overemphasize and exaggerate the results of breaking the rules. And, unfortunately, we tend to criticize ourselves and others for breaking the rules.

All of us would like to succeed at every task we undertake. There is nothing wrong with that. Doing well feels good. But when someone converts this hope or preference into a need, then the unspoken rule, *I must succeed at everything all the time,* becomes part of that person's thinking. There is a difference between preferring to do well and thinking, I *must* do well. If I prefer to do well and then find I have failed at a given task, I might be concerned, disappointed, maybe a little sad, but it won't be that much of a problem. If I believe the rule, *I must always do well and succeed at everything all the time,* then when I do fail at a given task, I am angry at myself, ashamed, guilty, and even depressed. Converting the *preference* to do well to a requirement results in very stressful reactions.

Unspoken rules are often accompanied by all-or-nothing thinking. If I obey the rule, then I'm great. When I break the rule, I think I'm absolutely terrible. Thus, the person who is overly anxious about doing well will think that he's great when he has a good experience and will think that he's stupid or terrible when he does poorly. Those who live by the rule, *People should never disappoint me,* think of you as a great true friend as long as all is going well but conclude that you are no friend at all as soon as the first disappointment appears. This swinging to extremes in our thinking compounds our stress.

When we break one of our unspoken rules, we are apt to exaggerate or overemphasize its importance. If I don't have what I think I must have, then I'll think it's terrible to be without it—not disappointing or unfortunate to be without it, but *terrible*. The person whose rule is, *I must never make a mistake in public,* thinks it intolerable when that happens. The very prospect of making a public mistake induces anxiety. "I couldn't stand it; I couldn't live with myself." These are the exaggerated reactions to breaking unspoken rules. As a matter of fact, there are few things that we couldn't stand or live with if we had to.

Perhaps even more serious is the tendency to put down ourselves and others when unspoken rules are broken. We think less of ourselves and others for not living up to the demands that the rules imply. If your rule is, *I must never lose my temper,* then when you do lose it, you tell yourself that you are a bad or terrible person. If your rule for others is,

People must always anticipate my needs, then you think of them as bad or evil people when they don't.

How can we go about reducing the stress caused by these unspoken rules? First, become aware of them. As noted earlier, we often take these rules so much for granted that we hardly know they exist. Examine each stressful situation you experience, particularly those involving unpleasant emotions like anger, anxiety, guilt, or depression, and get at the unspoken rules behind your reactions. Look for the *musts* and the *shoulds*. Repeatedly ask yourself, "Why do I feel as I do in this situation? What demands am I making on myself? What demands am I making on others?" You may have to think about a situation for a while before discovering your unspoken rule, but after you have done it a few times you will become skilled at it. This is actually taking inventory of your unspoken rules, and you may want to review some of the suggestions on how to take inventory (see Method 1, "Take Inventory").

Second, examine the thinking that accompanies your rules. Help yourself gain perspective by noting the all-or-none thinking and the exaggeration that accompanies unspoken rules. See if, when you fail to live up to one of your rules for yourself, you think that you are therefore a terrible or a weak creature. Notice if you are strongly condemning of others when they don't live up to demands you place on them. Take careful note of any all-or-nothing thinking and exaggerated reactions.

Third, talk it over with others. Share your rules with them and get their reaction. Have them share their rules with you. Just speaking the rules out loud will help because that exposes their unreasonableness and allows us to cease taking them so much for granted. As you critically examine the rules of others, you will be better able to examine yours critically as well.

Fourth, challenge the rules. Ask yourself, "Why must I think this way? Who says that I must live up to this rule? Why must I demand this of myself? Why should other people do as I wish?" Another series of questions goes like this: "Is it terrible if I don't live up to my rules? Am I a failure if I don't always live up to the demands I place on myself? Are other people terrible if they don't do what I want or behave as I wish they would? Is it possible that my reactions are really overreactions?" Unfortunately, these rules often come from deeply held beliefs, and they won't be changed easily, but you can begin to challenge them and challenge them repeatedly.

Fifth, revise your rules. Substitute a reasonable, less harsh rule for the one you are now following. For example, suppose your rule is, *I must always do my best.* Behind that rule is usually the other one, *It would be terrible if I didn't do my best.* Make a more reasonable rule, such as, *I prefer to do my best. I feel better when I do my best, but it is okay to be human. It isn't so terrible when I fall short of my goal.* Here are several unspoken rules and their revisions:

Unspoken rule: I must never make a mistake in public. I couldn't stand it if people saw me doing something stupid.

Revised rule: I would prefer not to make a mistake in public, but if I do, it's not the end of the world. I won't like it when people see me make a mistake, but I can stand it.

Unspoken rule: People must think well of me. It would be terrible if others don't like me.

Revised rule: I would like it if others think well of me. I certainly wouldn't like it if they didn't. But if some people don't like me, I can live with that. Further, I can like myself even when someone else does not.

Unspoken rule: People should never disappoint me. People who disappoint me have no right to do so. Something is wrong with people who disappoint me.

Revised rule: Life is easier when people keep their promises and react as I prefer. I know that at times people won't do this. I accept their faults just as I hope they will accept mine. I can't expect others to be what I want them to be.

Unspoken rule: People should not ask me to do what I don't want to do.

Revised rule: I prefer that people not make unwanted requests, but I can't expect them to know what I want and don't want.

Generally, we revise rules to change the *musts* and *shoulds* to preferences, and we note that when things don't go our way, the result is a situation which we don't like but can live with, rather than terrible, horrible, and something we just can't stand. You can practice revising unspoken rules by completing Exercise 1 at the end of this unit.

Sixth, note the difference in thinking according to revised rules and the original unspoken rules. The second exercise at the end of this unit tells you how to do this. As you note how much better you feel about yourself and others when you think in terms of the revised rules, you'll find it easier to substitute those for your original unspoken ones.

EXERCISES

1.   Select four situations which are stressful for you. Specifically, select one resulting in anger, one resulting in guilt, one resulting in anxiety, and one other of any type. Describe each situation in a few sentences. Then think through each situation carefully, asking yourself, "Why do I react as I do?" Keep asking that

question until you discover the unspoken rule which contributes to your reaction. Remember that unspoken rules are sometimes difficult to uncover. Use the examples in the text to help you. Record the unspoken rule; then write out a revision of that rule which is more reasonable and less apt to result in stress for you.

Situation 1. Anger:_____

_____

_____

Unspoken rule:_____

Revised rule:_____

Situation 2. Guilt:_____

_____

_____

Unspoken rule:_____

Revised rule:_____

Situation 3. Anxiety:_____

_____

_____

Unspoken rule:_____

Revised rule:_____

Situation 4. Other:_____

_____

_____

Unspoken rule:_____

Revised rule:_____

2. Seat yourself comfortably in a chair, close your eyes, and imagine yourself in one of the situations described in Exercise 1. Fantasize about that situation for a few minutes, experiencing it as vividly as you can. Remind yourself of your revised rule and imagine yourself in the situation believing the revised rule rather than the original unspoken rule. Note how differently you react with this new rule. Repeat for all the situations in Exercise 1 and record your reactions below.

Reactions to this exercise:_____

_____

_____

_____

METHOD 8

USE STRESS ANTIDOTES

Our reactions to events are as much a source of stress as the events themselves. The way we view things that happen to us and the demands placed upon us have a great deal of effect on just how much stress we experience. Thus, much of our stress is the result of a certain way of thinking. We've already seen that one way to deal with stress-producing thoughts is to revise our unspoken rules; another way is to use stress antidotes.

A *stress antidote* (or *stress innoculation* as Daniel Meichenbaum, the idea's originator, calls it in *Cognitive Behavior Modification*) is a carefully worded statement that replaces a stress-producing thought with a calming one. Thinking is a type of self-talk, and since we cannot focus on two thoughts at the same time, repeating a stress antidote forces other thoughts from our minds. In this way we eliminate the type of self-talk that adds to our stress. The more we can substitute calming self-talk for stress-producing self-talk, the better we can respond to difficult situations.

Suppose, for example, that a friend of yours does something that makes you very angry. Maybe he broke a promise to you, and while you're justly annoyed by his actions, your anger toward him makes you feel even worse. You experience not only the frustration of a broken promise but also the unpleasantness that comes from being angry. How could you respond to this situation without the interference of such anger? You could respond by saying to yourself, "So this friend is the type who breaks promises. OK, I can live with that without getting upset." Think of a job evaluation in which your supervisor prepares a report on how well you are doing. You haven't seen the report yet and are quite concerned about what it says. You can reduce your anxiety about this evaluation by using a stress antidote: "No matter what the report says, I can handle it if I stay calm and try to be objective."

Some people are stressed when they find they have a great deal to do and little time in which to do it. They begin to panic as they look ahead and wonder if they will ever get their work done on time. A stress antidote for this situation might be, "I'll take one thing at a time. I do what's possible and deal with whatever comes. If I panic, I'll only make things worse." Lack of self-acceptance can be helped by the statement,

"I'm human and therefore imperfect. So is everyone else. I will not place unreasonable demands on myself."

You can develop a number of stress antidotes to deal with specific unwanted emotional responses. Thus, to help lessen your anxiety you can say:

> *Calm down. Take it easy. There isn't anything you can't handle.*
>
> *Easy now. Take it slowly. No situation need destroy you.*
>
> *Let's get a perspective on this. Things often aren't quite as important as they seem.*

Anger, as we noted when discussing unspoken rules, results from encounters with people or events that we don't like and thinking that, because we don't want certain things to happen they should not happen. In addition to revising our unspoken rules, we can lessen anger with stress antidotes, such as

> *No need to get angry at this. People will not always act as I want them to.*
>
> *People do not exist to live up to my expectations. Why get angry at people for being who they are?*
>
> *Anger does me no good. It makes me feel bad. Let me try a more reasonable response.*
>
> *Getting angry at reality does not help me deal with it. I'm not going to let this situation get the best of me.*

When facing a new situation where you don't know what will be expected of you try saying:

> *I've lived through other difficult situations. Certainly I'll get through this one.*
>
> *I can't be sure that what I'm doing is correct since I don't know what is expected. I'll just do the best I can.*

In addition to these more general antidotes, you can work out others for specific situations you face. The exercises at the end of this unit help you do this and also provide you with the experience of using antidotes. While general antidotes are useful, those which you develop for your own personal circumstances are best.

Stress antidotes work best when carefully worded. Make them as brief as possible. Word them positively. That is, rather than saying, "I will not be afraid . . ., say, "I will be calm. . . ."

Keep your antidotes reasonable. Rather than saying, "I'm always on top of all situations," or "I know everything will work out just as I want," say, "I can handle whatever comes." Write your stress antidotes out on a card or paper and either memorize them or keep the written material with you.

Stress antidotes cannot be used carelessly or mechanically. They are not magic, and thoughtlessly repeating a simple statement does not do much good. Think about your stress-producing self-talk and ask yourself if you can't find a more reasonable way to approach the situation. Work out your stress antidote as a careful response to a difficult circumstance. The stress antidote can be helpful if you believe it, or, at least, if you consider it a reasonable alternative to your current thinking. When you take it seriously, then it has its effect.

A particular type of stress antidote is the *presleep suggestion*. This is a stress antidote that is repeated slowly and carefully twenty times before going to sleep. After you have done all you need to do before going to sleep and are lying back to allow sleep to come, you are in a state of mind that is particularly amenable to suggestion. Take your stress antidote and repeat it slowly and carefully; then touch the bed with the little finger of your right hand. After the second repetition, touch the bed again with the ring finger of your right hand. After each successive repetition, keep moving across your right hand and then across the left, starting with your left thumb and moving to the little finger of your left hand. Then reverse the process and when you return to the little finger of your right hand, you have completed twenty repetitions. Repeat this procedure each night for a week, being sure to stay awake for the entire process. After the first week, you can follow the same procedure except that you need not force yourself to stay awake. If you repeat the statement slowly and carefully and fall asleep before you are through, that is all right. Continue the process until you feel that the statement is a part of your thinking. Use only one presleep suggestion at a time.

The presleep suggestion can be very effective. It takes time and effort but is well worth it. Many people have reduced their stress using the stress antidote as a presleep suggestion. People who have experienced a fear of public speaking, for example, have been helped by the statement, "I am calm and confident when speaking in public." Why this method works is still a mystery, but when directions are followed carefully, the presleep suggestion is a very useful technique.

EXERCISES

1. Select at least three situations which are stressful for you. Describe each one in a few sentences. Using the directions and examples given in the text, write out a carefully worded stress antidote for each situation.

Situation 1: _____

_____

_____

_____

Stress antidote: _____

_____

_____

Situation 2: _____

_____

_____

_____

Stress antidote: _____

_____

_____

Situation 3: _____

_____

_____

_____

Stress antidote: _____

_____

_____

2.   Seat yourself comfortably in a chair, close your eyes, and imagine yourself in one of the situations described in Exercise 1.
Fantasize about that situation for a few minutes, experiencing it
as vividly as you can. Then calmly and carefully repeat your
stress antidote for that situation. Note the effect the antidote has
on your reaction. Repeat this for the other situations in Exercise
1 and record your reactions below.

_____

_____

_____

_____

_____

3.   Select the stress antidote which deals with your most stressful
situation and, following the directions in the text, use it as a
presleep suggestion for at least two weeks, longer if you wish.

Then repeat with the other stress antidotes, remembering that you should be using only one presleep suggestion at a time. Record your reactions to this exercise.

Reactions to this exercise: _____

_____

_____

_____

_____

_____

4. Print or type three significant stress antidotes on 3 × 5 cards. Post them on your mirror or carry them with you and review them carefully at least once a day.

METHOD 9

TOLERATE UNCERTAINTY

Generally, the more ambiguity or uncertainty in a difficult situation, the more stressful it will be for us as we attempt to deal with it. The prospect of being interviewed for a job is stressful for most people, but when we have no idea what will be asked in that interview, what qualities the person is looking for, or what is expected of us, that interview provokes even more anxiety. Retirement is a challenge in and of itself but is even more difficult to consider when the prospective retiree has no idea of what retirement is like, of what the financial picture will be, or at what age retirement will be possible. Whenever we can, we should try to reduce uncertainty by seeking information and taking appropriate action. This qualifies as working on the task and is discussed in Part III (Method 17, "Reduce Uncertainty").

Many times, however, our questions cannot be fully answered, at least for the moment. When that happens, we must learn to tolerate uncertainty. Suppose you are preparing a report: you have asked about what is expected; you have had all directions clarified; you have read earlier reports to see what is and is not acceptable—maybe you have eliminated 80 percent of the uncertainty. Excellent! But there is still that residual 20 percent. You still can't be absolutely sure that what you are doing meets the demands or expectations of others. That's the uncertainty that you must learn to tolerate.

Some people, fortunately, have little difficulty in facing uncertainty or tolerating ambiguity; some, however, find that their stress increases as uncertainty and ambiguity increase. They become frightened or upset whenever they find their questions unanswered. They find the very existence of uncertainty painful. When that happens, some unfortunate effects follow, the most frequent of which is known as *premature closure*. That term refers to the tendency for someone to jump to a conclusion and to stick to it firmly when there is no sound basis for that conclusion. It's as though the person reasoned, "Since there is no answer to my question and since I cannot tolerate that fact, I'll make up an answer and stick to it. That way, I'll have the confidence that comes with the certainty of knowing." Such people feel more comfortable with any answer—even a wrong one—than with the state of uncertainty.

A young man, unable to tolerate the uncertainty in a relationship with a young woman, may decide that she just doesn't care for him and therefore ends the relationship. Maybe she did care for him, but he couldn't handle the uncertainty and therefore exchanged it for the certainty of no relationship at all. Many people find themselves confused about values and morals. The more they think about the great questions of life, the more uncertainty they find. At times a person thinking about various religions and philosophical systems (questions of liberalism versus conservatism, changing sexual customs, or competing political systems) becomes confused and anxious. The experience of not knowing or of not being able to take a firm stand on life's great issues is so frightening and threatening for some people that they flee from the uncertainty and embrace a rigid, unthinking system that claims to give all the answers and remove all doubts. Thus, many people convert to rigid, doctrinaire religious or political systems because then they don't have to think anymore. They are spared the anxiety of making decisions. All of the answers are handed to them, and they find security in that certainty. Of course, none of this questions the validity or usefulness of any religious or political system. Nor do we say that all adherents of particular systems are simply fleeing ambiguity. The thoughtful adoption of any world view is the prerogative of any person. It's the unthinking flight to certainty as a means of dealing with the stress of ambiguity that is our concern here.

How does one learn to tolerate ambiguity? The first step is to recognize the need to do it. Accept the fact that there will be times when, no matter how hard you try, you will not be able to learn all you wish to know about a given situation. There are some questions that you will not have answered and some issues that you will not have clarified. At such times, the most reasonable approach is to recognize the need to tolerate the uncertainty.

Next, you can ask yourself, "Why not live with some uncertainty? Why do I have to know?" As you explore your own thinking, you may well discover that you have been assuming that uncertainty is inevitably upsetting and that certainty is always necessary—and you can learn to think otherwise.

Third, you must work on giving up the rule, I must be certain. That is a rule we cannot live by, a demand we cannot place on life. We can give that rule up if we deliberately and conscientiously set out to do so. (Refer again to Method 7, "Revise Unspoken Rules").

Fourth, look at the advantages of uncertainty and recognize that uncertainty is often the price you pay for some benefit you enjoy. For example, at times I have assigned a paper in a class and told the students they could write on any subject they liked so long as their papers related to the course material. Their initial enthusiasm for this assignment often became anxiety as they wondered, "Is my topic appropriate? Is my paper long enough? Inevitably, some students would say, "We'd feel much better if you would tell us exactly what you want us to do." My response was, "The price of freedom is uncertainty." The students could not be free to pick a topic of their own choosing without inviting some uncertainty. Some of the most exciting jobs possible are those which allow us to use our energy and resources as we choose. We can welcome uncertainty in our work when it means we are free to do as we wish. Uncertainty which brings these advantages can certainly be tolerated.

EXERCISES

1. Think of a situation facing you that has some uncertainty that cannot be reduced at the present time. Think of the lack of information and knowledge, the unfamiliarity, or the ambiguity that must be tolerated, at least for the time being. Record this information in the spaces provided.

    Situation:_____
    _____
    _____

    Areas of uncertainty:_____
    _____
    _____
    _____
    _____

    Now ask yourself the following questions, thinking through each one carefully, and recording your answer to each in the space provided.

    What can you say to yourself to help recognize the necessity of tolerating this uncertainty?
    _____
    _____
    _____

    Although you may want to reduce this uncertainty, is there any absolute need for you to do so? Can't you continue on even if uncertain?
    _____
    _____
    _____

What is the worse thing that can happen if you don't reduce this uncertainty? Can you tolerate this worse consequence?

_____

_____

_____

Can you give up the rule, *I must be certain*? Why?

_____

_____

_____

Does the uncertainty in this situation, in spite of its difficulties, have any advantages for you?

_____

_____

_____

2.   A stress antidote is a carefully worded statement which reduces stress by replacing a stress-producing thought with a calming thought. One stress antidote for dealing with uncertainty would be, *I find uncertainty uncomfortable, but I can live with it. I would prefer no uncertainty, but I can tolerate some uncertainty.* In the space below, write out your own stress antidote for the situation you recorded in Exercise 1.

Stress antidote:_____

_____

_____

_____

_____

METHOD 10

ANTICIPATE CHANGE

A *stressful situation* is defined in this guide as one which evokes a reaction of displeasure or discomfort within us. Certain characteristics of situations increase the possibility that we will find them stressful. In the last unit, the effect of uncertainty in contributing to stress was discussed. Another characteristic of a situation which makes it more stressful is suddenness or unexpectedness. When we are caught off guard or by surprise by even a small problem, our stress is increased. Seeing that the tires on my car are wearing out is one thing; have a tire fail when I least expect it is another. Going to work on a day when I know there will be interruptions is one thing; being interrupted when I don't expect it is another. Things which happen suddenly and unexpectedly are more stressful than events that we anticipate; learning to anticipate change reduces the probability of being caught by surprise.

We increase our stress if we unthinkingly assume that the future will be just like the past. How foolish to assume that my current supervisor will always be working with me or that a new supervisor will have the same policies as the present one. Parents who have more than one child can tell you it is a mistake to assume that the second or third child will behave the same way as the first. As the years pass by, your spouse will change. Activities which you once did together may lose their attractiveness. In recent decades, many women have changed their idea of what it means to be a woman in today's world—much to the surprise of many husbands. And, of course, you too can change. Your interests, your values, your goals are not always the same at age forty as at twenty.

Think of the many changes that we have experienced in our country since the 1960s: the civil rights movement, the women's movement, the sexual revolution, the change in our thinking about energy, inflation. You can complete this list yourself. Who would have thought, years ago, that large automobile companies would be in financial difficulty or that a baseball season would be halted by a strike?

There are changes in your future as well. We already know that the continued growth of computers and related technology will revolutionize the communications industry. The way your job is structured today may change. Ideas about how to raise children or relate to others will undoubtedly change. You and I will be doing things and thinking thoughts ten years from now that may surprise us.

As important as change on a national scale is, it is not as significant to you as changes unique to your life. The exercise for this method asks you to think of particular situations that you face and to anticipate what changes might occur. These changes can be pleasant or unpleasant. If you develop the habit of expecting change, of not putting your sense of security in the assumption that everything will stay the same, then you will anticipate change and thereby reduce its suddenness and unexpectedness.

EXERCISE

Below are listed several important areas of life (and places for you to list additional ones). In the space provided, list ways in which each area could change in the coming weeks, months, or even years.

Your job: _____

_____

Your family: _____

_____

Your friendships: _____

_____

Your finances: _____

_____

Your health: _____

_____

Other: _____

_____

Other: _____

_____

_____

METHOD 11

DEVELOP COMPETENCIES

Living successfully in today's complicated world requires the development and use of a very large number of competencies. Think for a moment of all the competencies you utilize every day—all of the things you have learned to do successfully. Further, think of the stress that comes when you find yourself in a particular situation for which you lack a needed competency. The homeowner who doesn't know how to make minor repairs around the house is at the mercy of others more skilled than he. The woman who doesn't know how to make friends will be more lonely than others. The teen-ager who doesn't know how to dance or to play a sport is at a real disadvantage in social situations and will suffer because of this.

A competency is a skill or body of knowledge that helps us in our daily living. Competencies are not limited to talents (playing the piano) or highly specialized skills (glassblowing) but include any of the hundreds of skills used everyday. Knowing how to shop for the best bargain is a competency. Knowing how to study for an exam is a competency. Knowing how to tell a joke is a competency.

Take, for example, the simple matter of keeping ourselves and our surroundings clean. Imagine a visitor from some other planet visiting a supermarket for the first time, looking for cleaning materials. If clothes are to be washed, one must look at one set of materials. If you are washing your body, there is another shelf with soap for that purpose, except of course, for your hair, which has another array of products. None of the products thus far will work on your car. There are still others for your floor, windows, shoes, etc.

If you decide to clean your clothes, you must then choose between liquid and powdered detergents; those with and without phosphates; those with and without bleach; those with and without water softener—and many other choices. For washing your body there are soaps with deodorants, those with other ingredients, and those that claim not to be soap at all. To keep yourself and your surroundings clean, you have to know about hundreds of products and the uses for each. You know which of the things are best cleaned by which materials. Washing a wool sweater requires different knowledge than that used in washing sheets; keeping leather products in shape is different from shining shoes. We could continue on with this illustration for pages, but the point has been made: keeping ourselves and our surroundings clean requires knowing about a wide variety of cleaning substances, shopping for them, knowing when and how to use them, and using them properly.

The use of cleaning substances is an insignificant part of life for most of us: I don't know of anyone who complains of great stress because he doesn't know much about soap! I have given this illustration in detail, however, to illustrate how, even when dealing with minor tasks in our lives, we utilize a considerable number competencies. In our society, the matter of keeping ourselves and our surroundings clean is very complex. Most of our daily living is also complex. How easy it is to overlook this important fact. The discussion of cleaning substances also helps us realize that many people experience stress because they lack a competency that others take for granted. Fortunately, that stress is reduced when the appropriate competency is learned.

Review the stressful situations in your life as listed in the inventory you completed earlier (Method 1, "Take Inventory"). As you review the following list of competencies, perhaps you will see a few that will help you deal with those stressful situations.

Writing a resume	Interviewing
Reading a bus schedule	Writing reports
Social skills	Handling anger
Speaking in public	Using a library
Delegating responsibility	Supervising a subordinate
Organizing materials	Listening
Chairing meetings	Managing time
Following directions	Getting along with others

The exercises at the end of this unit guide you in noting competencies you do have (which will help you develop the habit of thinking about competencies) and specifying needed competencies for specific situations. Once you begin to think in terms of competencies, you will ask yourself in any stressful situation, "What do I need to learn to do that will help me cope with this situation?" Once you have discovered the required competencies, you can begin to develop them. In looking for and developing needed competencies, you are also taking a problem-solving approach (Method 3).

Frequently when people review the stress in their lives, they discover that a considerable amount of their stress comes from the absence of a few important competencies. (Perhaps when you completed your own inventory, you discovered that much of your stress involved only a few key situations. What is the role of competencies in these situations?) In particular, people who lack the collection of competencies that constitutes assertiveness will experience considerable stress every day of their lives.

What do I mean by *assertiveness?* I have already referred to assertiveness as a collection of competencies. Being assertive means to (1) express your opinions and feelings; (2) behave appropriately whenever your needs or rights are being interfered with by the actions (or inaction) of others; (3) take initiative in satisfying your needs. Below is a list of some of the competencies that constitute assertiveness. As you review the list, note those things that you can and cannot do at the present time.

ASSERTIVENESS

Standing up for your rights

Expressing your opinion

Offering constructive criticism

Initiating conversations

Terminating conversations

Rejecting unreasonable criticism

Disagreeing with the opinions of others

Making your needs and wishes known to others

Accepting compliments

Giving compliments

Seeking out friends

Making suggestions

Saying "no" when appropriate

Asking for information

Telling others about yourself

I do not intend this to be an exhaustive list. This is a sampling of the many, many specific competencies which we require if we are to be assertive. You will note that being assertive involves the way we relate to and interact with other people. Since our lives and our well-being are so inevitably influenced by our relationships with others, improving those interactions is a very effective way of reducing stress.

Lack of assertiveness is a very common problem and the cause of a considerable amount of stress. Why are so many people reluctant or afraid to be assertive? Frequently, assertiveness is confused with aggressiveness. Some people suspect that being assertive means expressing uninhibited anger, being pushy, and insisting on your own way all the time. There is a difference between expressing your needs and feelings, on the one hand, and blowing up in anger, on the other. Being assertive enables you to make your point without being aggressive. Standing up for your rights when someone ignores them is not being pushy. Further, assertiveness involves being able to take the initiative in social situations, accept and give compliments, and engage in other activities having nothing to do with anger or aggressiveness.

Sometimes a person believes that being assertive means thinking highly of himself. If someone tells him that he looks especially nice today, he believes that he must respond, "Oh, this old suit. It's really cheap." Many women, after serving a delicious meal for which they prepared long and hard, think it immodest to accept sincere compliments. They find it difficult to say, "Thank you. I appreciate that." Is this response immodesty or honesty?

The unassertive person often assumes that she should not have to make her wishes known at all. If other people were as thoughtful as they should be, if they really cared, if they sincerely wanted us to be happy, they would know what we want. Your husband spends more time with his family than you think he should, but you don't express your concern. "If he loved me, he'd know how I feel." Is this reasonable? We need only to think about it for a minute or two to realize how unreasonable such thinking is. Even those who love us most are not aware of our every wish. They can know what we want and need only when we tell them.

Often unassertiveness results from fear of others. What if I tell my friend that I am unhappy with the fact that he constantly treats me like a child, always telling me what I should be doing? What if I say to the waiter, "This meal is not cooked properly: please take it back"? We have visions of our friend being enraged, of the waiter staring at us in shocked disbelief, and of everyone else being horrified at our behavior. If we look around us, however, we will see people behaving assertively all the time with the result that they get what they want without incurring these exaggerated reactions. Sometimes when we make a request of others, such as asking for change for a twenty-dollar bill in a store, the answer will be, "No." Submissive individuals fear this reaction, believing that encountering a refusal is an embarrassment or a humiliation instead of a normal event that we can learn to accept.

Another reason for unassertiveness is the lack of a sense of personal worth. Those who believe that their needs are unimportant, that they must surrender their wishes to those of others, or that they aren't "important enough" to have rights will certainly be unassertive. Sometimes this is a personality difficulty that requires considerable counseling or therapy to resolve.

There is another important reason why people fail to act assertively: *they don't know how.* They have never learned how to make simple, direct, unaggressive requests. They have never learned how to initiate a conversation. They have never learned how to refuse a request politely. As I pointed out when discussing the use of cleaning substances earlier in this unit, living requires the use of many competencies—often simple, obvious ones—and the lack of these competencies is at the root of much of our difficulty. Fortunately, the competencies required for assertiveness can be identified and learned.

What happens when we are not assertive? How do we get what we want? Unassertive people are often more aggressive than others since, lacking the skill to express their needs directly and simply, they believe they must fight to obtain what they need. Others suffer in silence, with their needs unmet. Another approach involves being manipulative or seductive. If we can't get what we want by asking for it, perhaps we can maneuver someone into giving it to us.

Let me emphasize that life requires us to be assertive. In our society, we expect people to take care of themselves, look after themselves, and to protect their rights. If you don't do it for yourself, who will? If you decide that you need to be more assertive (Exercise 3 at the end of this unit will help you make this decision), you can make use of a number of resources, such as books on assertiveness and assertiveness training workshops. This guide is not intended as a substitute for a complete assertiveness training program.

A final thought about competencies in general is that you will find it useful to think in terms of competencies rather than personality traits. That is, instead of thinking, "I am unassertive, or unable to get along with others, or always angry because I am that kind of person," try thinking, "I am unassertive, or unable to get along with others, or always angry because I haven't learned to be otherwise." We do not deny the reality of personality traits by emphasizing competencies. We make possible the opportunity to make changes in our lives when we think of skills that we can learn which will enable us to cope more successfully. Thus the first exercise at the end of this unit asks you to identify a few stressful situations and to specify what competencies will help you deal with that situation. Identify them, and then develop them. Frequently you will need some help in learning a new competency; at such times, you can learn to utilize resources (Method 20C).

EXERCISES

1. Take a few minutes to review all that you did yesterday. Examine each activity of the day, determine what competencies you utilized in that activity, and record them in the spaces below. Develop a list of as many competencies you utilized yesterday as you can. Don't overlook the obvious and include minor ones as well as major ones. Remember to think in terms of competencies instead of personality traits.

Competencies used yesterday:

_____	_____	_____
_____	_____	_____
_____	_____	_____
_____	_____	_____
_____	_____	_____
_____	_____	_____
_____	_____	_____
_____	_____	_____
_____	_____	_____

2. Select some situations which you find stressful. Describe each one briefly in the space provided. Review each one carefully and decide what competencies would help you deal with each situation more successfully. Record those; think about how you might develop some of them.

Stressful situation:_____

_____

_____

_____

Competencies which would be helpful:

_____	_____	_____
_____	_____	_____
_____	_____	_____

Stressful situation:_____

_____

_____

_____

Competencies which would be helpful:

_____	_____	_____
_____	_____	_____
_____	_____	_____

Stressful situation:_____

_____

_____

_____

Competencies which would be helpful:

_____   _____   _____

_____   _____   _____

_____   _____   _____

3. Review the material on assertiveness and note the examples of assertive behavior. Note those which you would find difficult. Also, keep a notebook with you for a week or two and note anytime you fail to be appropriately assertive, that is, anytime you are unable to take the initiative, express your feelings or opinions, or behave appropriately when your rights or needs were being interfered with by others. In the spaces provided below, indicate those assertive behaviors which you find difficult. Then describe how you would behave if you were to be appropriately assertive in each instance. Remember not to confuse assertiveness with aggressiveness.

Assertive difficulty:_____

_____

_____

Appropriate assertive behavior:_____

_____

_____

Assertive difficulty:_____

_____

_____

Appropriate assertive behavior:_____

_____

_____

Assertive difficulty:_____

_____

_____

Appropriate assertive behavior:_____

_____

_____

Assertive difficulty:_____

_____

_____

Appropriate assertive behavior:_____

_____

_____

Assertive difficulty:_____

_____

_____

Appropriate assertive behavior:_____

_____

_____

Seat yourself in a comfortable chair, close your eyes, and imagine yourself in each of these situations. First, imagine yourself behaving unassertively and them imagine yourself behaving assertively. When you have completed this imagining several times and you note that the image of behaving assertively is comfortable, select the assertive behavior which you believe would be easiest for you to perform and engage in that behavior each time you have the opportunity to do so. When you feel comfortable with that behavior, select the next easiest one for you and engage in it whenever you have the opportunity. Start with easy assertive behaviors, such as expressing opinions, before going on to more difficult ones. Continually add to your list of assertive difficulties as you discover them, working out and imagining the appropriate assertive behaviors, and engaging in those behaviors when you have the opportunity.

METHOD 12

SATISFY WANTS

All of us have a number of needs which we would like to have satisfied and experts agree stress occurs when we are prevented from doing so. When we cannot have what we want, we are frustrated, and that is a major source of stress. Consequently, an important way of reducing stress is to satisfy our needs.

What are your important wants or needs? What do you believe you need in order to have a reasonably happy, fulfilling life? There is no quick answer to that question—and certainly no complete one—but some thoughts probably come to your mind immediately. Obviously our basic physical needs must be satisfied. We have no life at all, much less a happy one, if we do not have sufficient air, food, and water. We also require adequate shelter from the elements. For most of us, fortunately, these basic physical needs are reasonably well satisfied.

Another physical need, the need for sexual activity, differs from the ones just discussed in that a person's life is not threatened when it is not satisfied. Nevertheless, it is a basic need and the extent to which we satisfy it is important in our lives.

The satisfaction of our psychological needs is equally important in determining how happy and fulfilling our lives are. All of us want to be loved. We want people to value us, to care for us, to cherish us. Signs of love and caring (someone spending time with us, enjoying our company, caring for us when ill, being considerate of our wishes) are enormously important and the person who believes that she is unloved is usually quite unhappy. The presence of friends and family in our daily lives can make the difference in how we respond to the needs and challenges of the day. Being loved is not enough; we also have a need to love. Caring for someone, expressing that care, helping those we love—all contribute to our inner sense of wholeness and satisfaction.

Eric Berne, in his book *Games People Play*, used the term *stroke* to indicate a unit of recognition. In his terminology, when someone smiles at us, responds to us favorably, or says a kind word to us, we are being stroked. Physical strokes, such as a back rub, are great, but Berne is talking more about psychological strokes through which we receive recognition from others. Without stroking, he argues, we shrivel and die.

Life is more fulfilling also if we have certain attitudes and feelings toward ourselves. The importance of self-acceptance, for example, has already been discussed earlier (Method 2, "Recognize Stress as Part of Life"). Self-respect and self-esteem involve valuing and caring for ourselves. What a difference it makes when we can view ourselves with pride and satisfaction. This does not mean that we ought to be smug or arrogant. Self-respect and self-esteem in a healthy individual do not constitute self-centeredness. In fact, to some extent, our ability to love others in a mature way requires that we have a reasonably good view of ourselves. Berne believes that self-stroking is as important as receiving strokes from others, and he notes, we are often quite stingy in this respect. Stroking yourself means being good to yourself, complimenting yourself, and rewarding yourself once in a while.

Psychologists have never agreed on a complete list of human needs. No one will quarrel with the statement that we all require food, water, and shelter and we all recognize the importance of love, recognition, and self-esteem. Beyond these, however, is a large number of human needs or wants that may or may not be part of everyone's life. We can forgo the debate about how universal these are and discuss a few to take note of some of the things we look for in our daily living. Take, for example, the desire to achieve. Most people take satisfaction, not in just doing something, but in doing it well. When we have accomplished a difficult task or done something that earns the admiration and respect of others, we feel good about it. Achievement is very important in our society.

We also have a desire to understand. We study the universe through science in order to improve our lives, but we also enjoy learning about the world around us because understanding is rewarding even if the knowledge we gain appears to have no immediate practical usefulness. Think of how upset you are when those around you behave in a way you do not understand. It is very unsettling when we have to ask ourselves, "Now *why* did he say that to me?" Understanding oneself is important too. Many people find it distressing when they are sad or upset and don't know why. Other wants include the desire for novelty, the desire for excitement, the ability to be able to predict and control what happens to us, and the need to know that we have an effect on others.

You may have noticed that I have spoken of both *needs* and *wants*. Psychologists speak of human needs. Psychological texts frequently include love, self-esteem, achievement, and others in a list of needs. Others, however, argue that while we certainly need a minimum of food, air, water, and shelter, all the rest constitute wants, i.e., while we do want them very much, we don't absolutely have to have them to live. Of course it is extremely important to know that one is loved, but a person can remain alive even when feeling unloved. Achievement may be important, but is it absolutely necessary? I find it helpful to use the term *wants* rather than *needs*. In fact, part of changing unspoken rules is to learn to think in terms of preferences rather than needs (Method 7, "Revise Unspoken Rules"). Thus, I have called this method *satisfy wants*.

Let's return to the question of stress by thinking of how stressed we are when these wants are not satisfied. If you want very much to achieve and you are prevented from doing so, you are stressed. If you are never challenged—and challenge is important to you—you are bothered by that lack of challenge. One common result of frustration is anger, a major sign of stress in our lives. A stressful reaction occurs whenever we are frustrated, whether the want being unmet is a major one, such as discussed thus far in this unit, or a minor one, such as missing a bus or being late for a meeting. While we can deal with minor frustrations in a variety of ways (several of the methods in this guide are appropriate here), the focus of this unit is on the major wants in your life. The exercise at the end of this unit directs your attention to major wants and shows you how to think about them in a way that helps you reduce stress in your life.

There are many reasons why our wants are often frustrated, some of them unavoidable. Often, however, our wants are unmet because we don't take the time to satisfy them. We become so involved in activities that consume our time that we neglect ourselves and our wants. At other times, circumstances change and, as a result, wants that used to be satisfied become blocked. Thus, our desire for status, security, and activity might be threatened when we face retirement if, until that point, our job has been the main means for satisfying those wants. Often, even our work and family do not satisfy all of our wants and we need to expand our range of activities and contacts to increase the chances of want satisfaction. At the same time, we can remember that not all wants will be satisfied and that the effort to satisfy every single want at all times will be frustrating and stress producing in itself. Resolve to seek reasonable satisfaction of your wants, accepting the fact that insistence on complete satisfaction is self-defeating.

Often people find themselves with a vague sense of frustration or unhappiness without really knowing why. They are so engrossed in their day-to-day living that they haven't stopped to think about satisfaction of wants, not realizing that at times we must plan actively for want satisfaction. Think of a recently retired person who finds life without work unfulfilling. He is unhappy, bored, and listless, wandering around the house with nothing to do. One step this person can take to improve his situation is to ask himself, "What important wants were satisfied by my work that are now left unsatisfied?" Two such wants might be the desire to achieve and to feel important. The next question is, "How can I go about satisfying those wants now, as a retired person?" If he then joins a volunteer organization, such as a church, a group working on behalf of retired persons, or a community action group, he will find work that is challenging and important and thus provide new sources of satisfaction for his wants. Similarly, all of us can systematically review wants in our lives and take steps to satisfy those which are currently unfulfilled. The first exercise for this unit will get you started on this important project.

EXERCISES

1.   In the spaces provided below, make a list of the major wants in
     your life. You can list some or all of those discussed in the text
     and add others that you consider important. List one on each
     line under *wants*. In the space after each want, under the head-
     ing *satisfaction*, put a number from 1 to 5 indicating the extent
     to which that want is satisfied in your life. 1 = not satisfied at
     all; 2 = satisfied very little; 3 = moderately well satisfied; 4 =
     quite well satisfied; 5 = completely satisfied.

WANTS   SATISFACTION

     Select five wants which you have marked 1 or 2 (or even 3 if the
want is very important to you). These five wants should be ones that
you would like to see satisfied more than they are now. Record each
want in the places provided below. Remind yourself that satisfaction of wants is important and that you have a right to seek satisfaction of your wants. Also remind yourself that you have to seek such
satisfaction actively.
     Taking these wants one at a time, think of a way in which each
one might be satisfied more than it is. What might you do to satisfy
this want? Where might you go? Would a change in the way you are
thinking satisfy that want? Who might help you satisfy that want?
Can you yourself satisfy that want (that is, can you do for yourself
what you are hoping others will do for you)? Review all of the ways
in which this want might be more fully satisfied. Select one or two
ways that seem to be more feasible and workable than others. Devise
a specific plan for increasing your satisfaction of that want. Record
that plan and your date for implementing that plan in the spaces
provided.

Want:_____ Plan for satisfaction:_____

_____

_____

Date for implementation:_____

Want:_____ Plan for satisfaction:_____

_____

_____

Date for implementation:_____

Want:_____ Plan for satisfaction:_____

_____

_____

Date for implementation:_____

Want:_____ Plan for satisfaction:_____

_____

_____

Date for implementation:_____

Want:_____ Plan for satisfaction:_____

_____

_____

Date for implementation:_____

2.   After you complete Exercise 1, you may conclude that there are some wants that cannot be adequately satisfied—at least for now. It may be that present circumstances make satisfaction of certain wants impossible. It may also be true that you choose not to do what you would need to do in order to satisfy a want.

You can help manage the stress that results from this lack of want satisfaction by reading certain other methods in this guide and including those wants in the exercises accompanying those methods. Those methods are as follows:

Method 2, "Recognize Stress As Part of Life"

Method 7, "Revise Unspoken Rules"

Method 8, "Use Stress Antidotes"

3.   Berne says that people also want stroking. We like it when people greet us with a smile, compliment us, remember us, praise us, etc. You can also stroke yourself. That is, you can do things for yourself that make you feel good: praise yourself,

reward yourself, treat yourself. List below five strokes that you can give yourself, and then work out a plan for how you will give yourself these strokes more often.

Ways to stroke myself:_____

_____

_____

_____

_____

Plan for more self-stroking:_____

_____

_____

_____

_____

METHOD 13

RESOLVE CONFLICTS

Another major source of stress for most of us is conflict. When we are forced to make the difficult choices that conflicts require of us, we often experience frustration, anger, anxiety, or worry. The energy we spend working on conflicts or just fretting about them contributes to our stress. Conflict—like change—is a natural part of life, and in times as complex as ours we experience conflicts regularly. Learning to resolve conflicts is a useful way of reducing stress.

Many conflicts result from competing demands for our time or attention made by the various people in our lives. A good friend wants us to spend time with him and a child asks that we spend time with her—and we must choose. A spouse expects certain behaviors from us, but a neighbor may have different expectations. Perhaps the most common source of conflict for many is the competing demands of family versus work. Most of us could spend all of our time either with our family or our work if we could, but we must respond to both, without neglecting either.

On the other hand, we also have our own needs. Sometimes we experience conflict when we attempt to respond to our own wants as opposed to demands from outside ourselves. Do I do what I want today, or do I complete my work? Do I spend my vacation where I please, or do I go where my family wishes? The problem of taking care of ourselves while responding to the demands and expectations of others can be a major one.

Choices involving values represent another major source of conflict. How do I respond to my belief about respect for life in a time of war? Should I follow my own values when all my friends want me to act differently? If acting on my values could hurt a friend, to which do I owe my allegiance: my values or my friend? How far do I go in protecting the rights of an individual at the expense of the group, and vice versa? How do I balance meeting the needs of today with planning for tomorrow? Many of our political, religious, and social problems can be understood as conflicts in values.

Decisions about how to utilize our personal resources also involve conflict. The problem of how we spend our limited time has already been mentioned. Since for most of us, money is also limited, decisions about its use leads to conflict. Shall we take a vacation or have the roof fixed? Shall we save our extra money or spend it? Do we put our money in a safe, low yield investment, or do we take a greater risk with the hope of higher yield?

Conflicts arising from competing demands, from differing values, and from using our personal resources are not the only ones we face, but they do represent major conflicts in our lives and illustrate the nature of conflict. Any attempt to list all the major sources of conflict would necessarily be incomplete.

Experts frequently divide conflicts into four major types. Sometimes we must choose between two alternatives, each of which we want very much. The problem is, we can't have both. Thus, if I have to choose between two delicious desserts, I am experiencing this type of conflict. Choosing between eating a sweet dessert and refusing it in order to protect my weight control program is another example. This type of conflict is usually resolved easily since once we have made our choice, we have something that we want and that is satisfying enough to make us happy with our decision.

At other times we must choose between two alternatives, neither of which we want. I can go to the dentist, or I can allow my teeth to get worse. I can pay my taxes, or I can get into trouble. Neither alternative is desirable, but one must be selected. This type of conflict is not as easily solved as the first since, when we make our choice, we get something or do something that we'd rather avoid. Fortunately, the pleasure that comes with resolving a conflict sometimes outweighs our unhappiness with the option we have selected.

Conflict also comes when we face a situation which we both like and yet dislike at the same time. A person who is offered a job which has a higher salary than her present job (the part she likes) but requires her to move to another part of the country (the part she doesn't like) experiences this type of conflict. The fourth and final type of conflict is when we face two such alternatives; that is, we have a choice between two alternatives and each one of them has something that we like and something that we don't like. Thus, if I were to be offered two jobs, each of which had advantages and disadvantages, I would experience this type of conflict. Conflicts involving situations which we both like and dislike at the same time are often difficult to resolve.

There is no simple formula for resolving conflicts, but we can do some things that will help us. We can best begin by deciding that we will make a choice. All too often we avoid making the choice and keep postponing our decision, thus increasing our stress and prolonging our difficulties. When we accept the fact that conflicts are a major source of stress and that resolving conflict can lessen our stress, we are more apt to work at ending our conflicts instead of postponing our decisions.

The essential nature of a conflict is that it presents us with a choice.

We can't have everything in a conflict situation—we must choose. Frequently conflicts are not resolved because we fail to face that simple fact. We can resolve our conflicts more easily if we recognize that a choice must be made; we must give up something we want or endure something that we don't want, and there is no other way out of the situation. Once we accept that we can't have everything and can't avoid all difficulties, we can then go on to make our decisions more easily.

Similarly, we must learn to accept the fact that we may make a mistake in our choice. The desire to avoid error—to be right all the time—can paralyze us and keep us from making choices. As long as we think, "What if I make the wrong choice?", we will have difficulty making any choice. We will resolve conflicts more easily once we accept the possibility that we might make an error—but that making no choice is the greatest error we could make. Can we give up the unspoken rule, *I must be right all the time?* (See Method 7, "Revise Unspoken Rules.")

We will also find it easier to make the choices necessary to resolve our conflicts if we learn to accept partial resolutions of our conflicts, realizing that sometimes no complete, final resolution is possible and that there is no right answer to our problem. This is another example of tolerating uncertainty (see Method 9).

Take the example of the person facing the decision of deciding how much time and effort to spend meeting her own needs versus meeting the needs of other people in her life. How much does one person sacrifice for the sake of family and friends? There is no one complete answer to that question. A person might make one decision today and a different one tomorrow. Each individual decision may seem not exactly right and one's lifetime may see many, many such decisions. Maybe that's the best one can do: in some instances, there will be no final decision that is always satisfying. The struggle with the issue will continue unless the person realizes that she has to live with an inexact, approximate solution. Our courts and legislatures will always struggle with the problem of the rights of the individual versus the rights of the group: the struggle will be less stressful if the people involved recognize that there is no one perfect solution out there waiting to be discovered.

Another approach to this same dilemma is to stop thinking that we must *find* the right answer, as though it were out there somewhere, and devote our efforts to *creating* a solution. There is no "correct" answer to many of our conflicts: *we* create our answer, and that answer is correct for us. As a free individual, I have the right to make choices which feel good to me, and I will experience less stress if I exercise that right rather than seek out some nonexistent correct answer that applies to all individuals in all circumstances. Change your thinking from, "What is *the* thing to do?", to, "What do I want to do?"

Since many conflicts concern values and competing demands on our time and resources, they may be more easily resolved if we clarify our values (Method 14) and establish clear priorities (Method 15A). The working man who decides that time spent each weekend with his children is a number one priority and more important to him than any career objective has an easier time deciding how to spend the weekend than his neighbor who hasn't made such a decision. Thus, once you work on your major conflicts, clarify your values, and establish your priorities, you will have a much easier time settling the little conflicts that come your way daily. Failure to do so means that you spend energy and time continually experiencing the same conflicts over and over again—and that only adds to your stress.

EXERCISE

Make a list of all the conflicts you experience over a short period of time: a few days or a couple of weeks. List every conflict, no matter how minor it may seem. You may want to carry a small notebook around with you and jot the conflicts down as they come to you. Describe each one in one sentence such as, "The decision to spend the evening studying versus going to a party." The list may be quite long; record them on a separate sheet of paper and then return to this exercise.

Study your list of conflicts. You will find that many conflicts are similar; look for the general areas or categories of conflict. Some may involve the use of time or money. Others will involve particular value choices. Perhaps a large number involve your job or schooling, or your relationship with particular people. Rewrite your list of conflicts, arranging them in categories. A given conflict may seem to belong in more than one category. In that event, put it in the one which seems most appropriate.

Decide the order in which you will work on the conflicts: Which category of conflicts would you like to work on first? Put the number 1 by that category. Then select the second, third, etc.

Follow the directions below for your number 1 category. Then follow them again for each of the remaining categories.

Review the conflicts listed in the category which you are now working. Select those conflicts which are relatively minor and which continue largely through your procrastination. Select a date in the near future by which you will make a decision for that conflict. Record that date next to the conflict and be sure to make a decision by that date.

The remaining conflicts in this category are those which are of greater importance to you. Select them one at a time and ask yourself the following questions:

What information do I need to help me make this decision and where can I find it?

Who can I ask for help?

What are the arguments for and against each alternative in the conflict?

Is any of the following keeping me from making my choice:

- The unwillingness to risk error
- The desire to have both alternatives and not to choose
- The unwillingness to accept a partial solution
- The belief that the answer is "out there" rather than in me

If there is information you can gain to help you, go get it. Talk with anyone whose advice you think will help you. Study the arguments, pro and con, for each alternative. Recognize and challenge the thoughts and demands which prevent you from making your choice. Then repeat the following statements (or some paraphrase of them) to yourself slowly and carefully, thinking of their meaning:

I know as much about this problem as I probably ever will. There is no perfect resolution to this conflict. I can't have it both ways, and I can't avoid the possibility of error. I can, however, create my own solution to this conflict and live with the consequences. Since this is preferable to continued conflict and its stress, I will make my decision.

Then make a decision, record it, and proceed to your next conflict.

Use this outline to help you:

Conflict:_____

_____

_____

Information needed:_____

_____

_____

Sources of help:_____

_____

_____

Arguments for first alternative:_____

_____

_____

_____

_____

Arguments for second alternative:_____

_____

_____

_____

_____

What keeps me from making the choice?_____

_____

_____

Decision:_____

_____

_____

METHOD 14

CLARIFY YOUR VALUES

You can begin thinking about the importance of values if you imagine what would happen if someone took a steel hammer and pounded on your thumb for a few minutes. No matter who you are or what your position in life, you would feel severe pain, and you would do whatever you could to stop the pounding. Certainly there is no doubt about that.

Now imagine that you have just been fired from a job. What is your reaction to this event? You can't predict that reaction as easily as when you felt the hammer on your thumb. If you see yourself as the family breadwinner and take pride in your on-the-job performance, you will probably be quite upset, even depressed, at being fired. If you see your loss of the job as one more evidence of a failing economic system and proof that people like you always get the short end of the stick, your response would more likely be anger or fear about the economic future. If you place little value on having a job at all, your response could be a very quiet one involving little emotional reaction.

This guide has often pointed out that our inner responses to events in our lives is important in experiencing how much stress we experience. One component of that inner reaction is our value system: our sense of what is important; our idea of what we want to do with our lives; our sense or lack of it, of meaning and purpose in life. Whereas as some stressful situations, such as being hit on the thumb with a hammer, will provoke a similar response in almost everyone, other situations, such as being fired, are interpreted by the person, and that person's value system will influence that interpretation. The extent to which many situations are stressful for us depends on the meaning of that event in the context of our value system. Your goals for yourself, your religious outlook, your philosophy of life, and your moral system—the term *values* in this guide refers to all of these—are an important consideration in any stress management program.

Think of people you have known who have experienced injustice or other suffering, such as serious illness or injury. Some respond with bitterness and anger; others with courage and heroics. Viktor Frankl, a Jewish psychiatrist imprisoned in a Nazi concentration camp during World War II, indicated that we can bear almost any circumstance if we have a sense of purpose and meaning in life. In fact, he considered the search for meaning in life to be fundamental in all of us. Frankl wrote movingly of how many of his colleagues found meaning in life even in their concentration camp existence. He, for example, found meaning by being of help and counsel to his fellow prisoners.

This is a somewhat extreme example; after all, when we talk about the stresses of everyday living, we aren't dealing with concentration camp existence. Nevertheless, we can see that our reaction to any situation we face in life, from minor annoyances to major tragedies, can be influenced by the way we interpret that event and the impact of that event on our value system. The pain of childbirth, for example, is more easily tolerated than pain inflicted by injury because of the importance placed on giving life. We can handle the stress of our job more easily if we see our work as meaningful and important. Our response to difficulties within our own families will be influenced by the value we place on family harmony. Those who counsel the dying often speak of how differently people respond to the prospect of their own death, and how one's values and sense of purpose are of enormous importance in determining that response.

Elsewhere in this guide I discuss setting priorities and making choices and decisions. People who are confused about their values and have no clear ideas about their lives find that they can't resolve conflicts or make decisions because they have no long-term view of life that gives meaning to their decisions. Since they have not made major decisions in life, each minor decision becomes a crisis. Those who know who they are and what they want from life can more easily deal with day-to-day decisions.

A complete program for dealing with stress, therefore, involves clarifying your values: thinking about what is important for you in your life in the long run. This means thinking about your philosophy, your religion and your morals. It means asking yourself about what is most important to you, what your goals and dreams are, and what you hope to do with your life. Clarifying your values means finding meaning in your life and thus in your daily activities. Then, when you face stressful circumstances, you will see them in a larger context, namely, that of your entire life, and that will enable you to deal with them more easily.

Clarifying your values is one of life's major tasks. It is never fully completed. Two periods in life that are most apt to be characterized by a clarification of values are adolescence and middle age. The adolescent is seeking values on which to plan her life. What occupation shall I enter? Am I seeking enjoyable work, money, fame, achievement? What am I seeking for my life anyway? When we reach middle age, we often pause to see how our life is going and ask, "Have I made the right choices? Now that I've been living this type of life for several years, is this what I really want? Would I do it differently if I could do it again? Do I want my children to live the same type of life that I am living?" While these two periods in life are particularly concerned with values, all of us at any point in our lives can examine our value system.

Since value clarification is a life-long task, no guide or exercise can do this work for you. You must do it yourself. My purpose in raising the subject is to point out the role that values have in our reactions to stressful situations, to help you realize how very important values are in our living, and to get you to start thinking about your values if you have not already done so. You can begin the process by realizing that this is an important task. Realize that you must decide what your values are and you must *create* meaning in your life rather than sitting back and hoping that someday you will discover it. The exercise at the end of this unit is provided to help you start your thinking. Complete it thoughtfully. It is one of the longer exercises in this guide, but as noted elsewhere, I have used these exercises in my work in past years and know that they are worth the time. The exercises get you started thinking or rethinking your values; you must go on from there. Discussions with friends, participation in religious groups, further reading, or enrolling in values clarification courses are a few of the ways you can continue the process. You may have seen the poster that reads, "Whether or not life is worth living depends on who is living it." That means clarify your values.

EXERCISES

1. Below is a list of values, each of which may or may not be important to you. The list is necessarily incomplete and some of the items overlap others. In the space provided, put an X next to each item which you consider important to you, which represents your values. There is no need to limit your choices; you may select only a few, or you may select all of them. Mark each one that is important to you.

   ____Pleasure/comfort

   ____Success in others' eyes (status/fame)

   ____Knowledge/wisdom/ understanding

   ____Love and friendship

   ____Plenty of leisure

   ____Excitement/adventure

   ____Security

   ____Self-respect

   ____Health

   ____Success in your own eyes

   ____Sacrifice for others

   ____Beauty

   ____Wealth

   ____Personal maturity and integrity

   ____Meaningful work

   ____Equality/justice

   ____Independence/freedom

   ____Happiness

   ____Helpfulness to others

Next, decide what values you have that are not in the above list. You can help determine these by asking yourself the following questions: What is really important to me in my life? If I had but one more year to live, what would I do? What would I be willing to spend time on? money on? to argue for? to die for? to join an organization for? Record your additional values in the spaces below.

_____

_____

_____

_____

_____

_____

_____

The final task is to select from the above lists (the one provided and the one you have created) the 16 values which are most important to you. Select 16 from the lists above which you value more than the others and record those in the spaces below. Use words which best express the value as you understand it; you need not use the exact wording in the list that was provided. Think these through carefully and record your 16 most important values (without being concerned about any particular order).

My 16 most important values:

_____   _____

_____   _____

_____   _____

_____   _____

_____   _____

_____   _____

_____   _____

_____   _____

2.   On the next page you will find 16 lines arranged in a particular pattern. In this exercise, you will take the 16 values you have listed above and record them in order of importance to you. Look over the 16 values and select the three or four which seem most important to you. Study these few and then decide which is _the most important value_ to you. Never mind anyone else's opinion—all that counts here is what you think. Record that value on the line at the top of the page next to number 1. Now place the next *two most important values* to you (looking at the few you have already selected) on the lines to the right of number 2. Now select those three or four values which you believe are *least* important to you. Since they are your values, they are all important, of course, but now you must decide which are less important than others. Study these few and decide which is *least important of all* and record that one in the space at the bottom of the page to the right of number 7. Then record the next *two least important* on the lines to the right of number 6. Now look at the values remaining. Study them and decide which of the three remaining ones are *more* important than the others and record those three on the lines to the right of number 3. Study the seven remaining values; decide which three of those seven are *less* important than the others and record those in the spaces to the right of number 5. You now have four values remaining; record those in the spaces to the right of number 4.

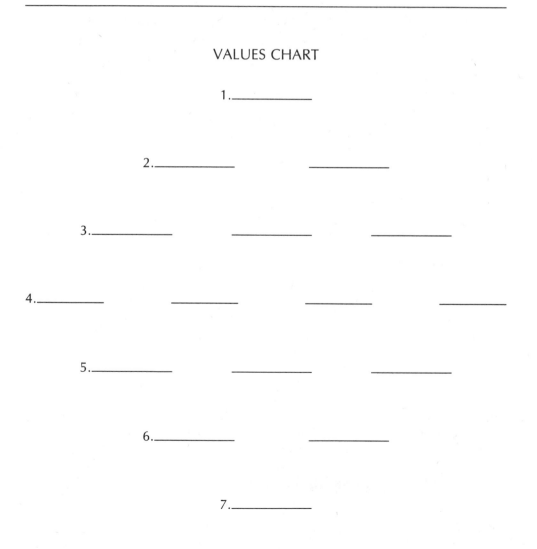

VALUES CHART

1._____

2._____   _____

3._____   _____   _____

4._____   _____   _____   _____

5._____   _____   _____

6._____   _____

7._____

PART III

WORKING ON THE TASK

The stress we experience results from our reactions to the tasks and events we encounter in our daily living. In Part II you learned how to modify your reactions to tasks and events; in Part III you will learn how to work on the task itself. In his book *Contemporary Psychology and Effective Behavior*, James Coleman points out that frustrations, conflicts, and pressures are major sources of stress, and the number of demands, their ambiguity, and their suddenness combine with the characteristics of the person (such as the person's way of looking at the problem and his or her level of competence) to determine how much stress is experienced. Part III discusses how you might work on the task in a way that will reduce your stress.

METHOD 15

REDUCE DEMAND

When most people are asked about their stress, they talk about the pressures that they are under. Our typical image of the stressed person is that of someone with a great deal to do, rushing from activity to activity, feeling hassled and frantic, trying to complete work in the time available. Sometimes the stressed individual is seen as one who shoulders considerable responsibility and who must make important decisions. This way of looking at stress emphasizes the external component of stress: the demands placed on us. When stress results from too many demands or from having particular types of demands, we can reduce stress by reducing the demands.

This does not mean that there is a direct relationship between the amount of demand on us and the degree of stress experienced. Since stress results from our inner reaction to external demand, we may feel little stress even when we face many demands so long as our reaction to those demands is not one of anxiety, worry, and similar emotions. People differ in their response to external demands—some seem to thrive on having a great deal of work to do. Those who work with enthusiasm, engage in many family activities, and involve themselves in community affairs often enjoy this level of activity and would not describe these demands as stressful at all. In fact, they would find the elimination of this activity as stressful. Others, however, do find that excessive demand or limited time in which to complete their work is stressful. Further, we frequently discover that a particular task or responsibility, while not excessive, is very stressful for us.

Review the stress in your own life as noted in your inventory (Method 1). How much of it comes from demands placed on you? In addition to altering your response to those demands by using the methods already discussed, you can also work to reduce the number of demands.

Reducing demand is not always easy or even possible. Some demands come with our job, for example, and we are obligated to meet them. But others are self-imposed and so much a part of our way of living that we are reluctant to give them up. Often when we say that we can't stop any of the things we are doing, we sometimes mean that we *won't* stop anything we are doing. A careful review of the demands to which we are responding shows that some of those demands can be reduced. As you complete your review, ask yourself if you are trying to do too much. Must you do everything that you are trying to do? Are there self-imposed demands which might be reduced? An honest attempt to answer such questions helps you find where demand can be reduced.

15A—ESTABLISH PRIORITIES

Reducing demand by eliminating activities can be difficult. Sometimes we want to do everything and find the prospect of eliminating any activity unpleasant. We can help ourselves in this effort by establishing priorities. We must think through all that we are trying to accomplish and decide what things are more important than others. If we do this thoughtfully, we can then more easily give up activities of lower priority.

Women who entered the work force after being married and bearing children find it difficult to keep up with the demands of both work and family. The pressure (and guilt) they feel in such situations can be painful. Experience has shown that women who managed this new situation best were those who did not try to be the complete career woman and the complete homemaker at the same time. That is too much to ask. Instead, successful women selected their career or homemaking as their number one priority. They fulfilled the demands of the number one priority as much as possible and responded to the demands of their second priority as time allowed. This does not mean that women who chose a career as number one priority neglected or ceased to care for their families. It means that they accepted the fact that they would not be as complete homemakers as they would like. They even established priorities within the various responsibilities of homemaking—for example, deciding to spend their time with the children and let entertaining and housekeeping take less of their time. If they had to entertain less or keep a less-than-perfect house, that was okay—because they were sticking to their clear priorities.

None of us can do all that we want. Consequently, we have to decide what is most important for us and concentrate on that. First, we must learn to sort out important from unimportant demands. When we find that we cannot do all we would like to do in a given period of time, we can decide what demands are important and what can be left unmet. You may decide that taking your child to the zoo is clearly more important than finishing the housework, and since you cannot do both, the housework is set aside. Second, we can help ourselves if we learn to separate major tasks from details. We can address ourselves, for example, to the task of keeping up on the news without worrying about each detail of every story.

Some priorities are lifelong or nearly so, for example, our commitment to family or career. We should also make our physical and mental health a lifelong priority. From time to time, our short-term priorities change. When we're physically exhausted and run-down, rest takes priority over work or recreations; at other times these priorities are reversed.

Once we have established our priorities, we can set out to work on our tasks one at a time. Start with the first priority, then the next, and so on. (See the exercises at the end of this unit.) In fact, even without going through all the work of establishing priorities, we help reduce stress by making a list of tasks needing completion and working on that list, one item at a time. If you find yourself unable to give up items of low priority, perhaps you are living by the unspoken rule, I must always complete every task. If this is the case, then you want to learn to replace that rule with a more reasonable one (see Method 7, "Revise Unspoken Rules").

15B—ELIMINATE SOME ACTIVITIES

We can eliminate some of the demands we face even without being concerned with overall priorities. Whenever you can eliminate some activity in an overloaded schedule, you are decreasing demand and thereby reducing a source of stress. Many people, for example, work very hard at their jobs and then try to crowd a complicated social life into evenings and weekends. A simpler social life might be of advantage for a while. Other people have many different projects going at one time; they might better confine their efforts to a few. In any circumstance, ask if you must do everything you are trying to do or if you might easily eliminate some of your activities. You may find that while you have assumed that everything you are doing is essential, in reality you can abandon some of those activities without any problem.

15C—MAKE ACTIVITIES LESS COMPLEX

When you are about to begin a very large project, the prospect of having to complete a great deal of work may be stressful in itself. Often we worry about particularly complex assignments. We can make these assignments less complex if we break them into parts and work at each part individually. A person making a long-range plan for a corporation, for example, might find the task easier to approach by outlining its component parts: gathering data, interviewing people, establishing goals, ordering the goals, setting timetables for achieving goals, and so on. Planning a meal for several guests might appear less difficult if we think about each course or type of food to be served separately as well as by concentrating on the various parts of this task: selecting the menu, making the shopping list, shopping, cleaning house, preparing some food the day before the meal, and so on. If we can learn to look at the various parts of our task without, of course, losing sight of the entire picture, we can then focus on one task at a time. Instead of being distressed about the complex task in front of us, we can say, "Now what is the next step? What is the one thing I must do today?"

15D—SCHEDULE DEMANDS

There are times when we want to reduce the number of demands but cannot eliminate many of them completely. We may be able to schedule those demands so that we don't have to deal with too many of them at any given time. The person who does the Christmas shopping early is applying this principle in a very practical way. The student who keeps up with a study schedule and completes term papers before the crush of finals week is scheduling demands so that they do not all come at once. People experiencing intense grief may want to postpone major decisions until a later time. The decision to schedule demands means we must fight the temptation to postpone every task until we absolutely have to do it. When we do that, we then have no choice but to take work as it comes. If we keep up with our demands, we can gain some control over them and schedule them to make our lives more comfortable.

15E—REFUSE UNREASONABLE DEMANDS

Considerable stress results from our tendency to meet demands, often unreasonable ones, that are imposed on us by other people—sometimes without their being aware of it. Melvin Gurtov once stated, "Looking back, I see that for most of my life I lived and worked in accordance with other people's dreams and expectations. Now I claim my time."[1] Most people associated with us have some idea of how we should behave or what we should think. They let us know, in both obvious and subtle ways, just what they expect of us. We can run into difficulty when we unthinkingly accept those demands and attempt to meet the expectations of others. Frequently people spend an enormous amount of time and energy trying to be what someone else wants them to be. When others do not accept us as we are but instead insist that we be different, then we run the risk of denying our needs in an attempt to meet theirs.

[1]Gurtov, M. *Making Changes: The Politics of Self Liberation.* Oakland: Harvest Moon Books, 1979.

Ironically, the demands others place on us are often unreasonable and sometimes impossible to meet. Few students, for example, are perfect, and those who try frantically to live up to their teacher's expectations of perfection have a hard time. The same is true of children, parents, supervisors, and employees. The other person may not openly say, "You must be this or that" and, in fact, may even deny that they are making a demand, but we know the demand is there. Often the demands of different people contradict and compete with one another, and we find ourselves caught in the middle. Teen-agers often find that they can't be the son or daughter their parents want and be the type of person their friends want at the same time. The more they try to please everybody, the less they please anyone. Use Exercise 3 of this unit to think about demands placed on you by others.

Even worse is the situation where one person gives us contradictory demands. Sometimes young adults have received these messages from a parent:

A. Go out and get married.

B. Stay home and take care of me.

A. Succeed.

B. Don't do better than I.

(Theorists in transactional analysis write a great deal about such messages.) These are "no win" situations: no matter what we do, the other person won't think we've done the right thing. If someone complains that when you elect him to chair a committee, you are giving him too much work to do, and if you don't elect him, you are telling him you don't like him—you can't win! You can reduce stress considerably at these times by refusing this unreasonable demand and saying to yourself, "I will not let people put me in such predicaments; I will not attempt to do the impossible. If there is no way I can win, I'll just do the best I can and not worry about it."

Sometimes refusing a demand is as simple as not accepting a task which is unreasonable or impossible. I was once asked to give a twenty-minute talk on how to reduce stress. I refused, saying that such a large topic could not possibly be covered in twenty minutes. Instead, I talked about one specific way to reduce stress. Instead of agreeing to requests that put us in impossible situations, we must learn not to accept such demands in the first place.

None of this means that we aren't concerned about requests that others make of us or that we should be indifferent to the expectations that others have for us. Responding to expectations of parents, teachers, and supervisors can be a way to learn and to grow. Of course, we want to be sensitive to the wishes of significant people in our lives. The difficulty comes when we strive so much to live up to other's expectations that we neglect our own needs and wishes or when the expectations of others are so unreasonable and contradictory that they cannot possibly be fulfilled.

15F—REDUCE SELF-IMPOSED DEMANDS

The expectations of other people are not the only source of unreasonable demands. We frequently impose such strong demands on ourselves that we experience excessive stress. Sometimes we do this thinking that the demand comes from others, not realizing that we are the unreasonable taskmasters.

Take, for example, the perfectionist. This person needs to do everything in the absolutely best possible way. The desire to do a task well and competently is nothing compared to the demand that perfectionism places on us. Thus, our supervisor asks for a written report, and we fret and struggle because we have decided that we must write the best and most complete report ever written. Well done is not enough. For every student who studies too little there is another anxiety-ridden student who overstudies, making himself virtually memorize the text. The ambitious and the hard-working are to be commended, but those who force themselves to meet impossible standards are not being reasonable with themselves.

For some people, it's not perfectionism but some other demand that causes the difficulty. A person who demands of herself that she never waste any time experiences frustration and regret—even guilt—on every occasion that some time is wasted. If she could reduce the demand and attempt to be as efficient as possible while realizing that everyone wastes some time once in a while, then she can better handle those inevitable moments when she is not working at full efficiency.

One frequent self-imposed demand that gets us into trouble is the implicit demand to please everyone. A person who resolves never to disappoint anyone, never to be different from what others wish him to be, and never to get anyone angry at anyone is in for a difficult time. Not everyone you know will like you. You will not win everyone's approval. The attempt to please everyone increases stress. Earlier we discussed the demands that others place on us. Now we can see that another problem is the tendency to demand of ourselves that we meet those other demands. We need not.

There is one type of self-imposed demand that causes considerable unhappiness: the often unspoken self-demand that we do for others what only they can and must do for themselves. Suppose you have a friend or relative who has a pain in her mouth but won't go to a dentist. You offer reasons why good dental care is needed and why postponing the inevitable is foolish. She still doesn't go. You argue some more; you beg and plead—but she won't go. If you do all that you can reasonably do and then accept the fact that she won't seek dental help, you are in a manageable situation. If, on the other hand, you decide that you must make her go, you may be putting yourself in an impossible situation. Only she can decide to go to the dentist. You can do your part as any friend would, but you must leave to her what only *she* can do.

Sometimes a friend is depressed, and we decide to help him feel better. That commendable effort will turn to an unreasonable self-imposed demand if we feel that we *must* make him feel better. If we judge our efforts by how hard we tried, then we can feel good about what we have done. But if we judge our efforts by whether or not the other person responds, we might feel that we have failed, even in a situation where there was no chance of succeeding.

This is not to say that we should not attempt to help other people. In fact, helping others helps us as well as them. The danger to avoid is the tendency to do for others what they must do for themselves. We can offer our help and assist in anyway possible—and then respect the other person's freedom to feel and respond as they wish.

This discussion of demands illustrates how our inner response interacts with external demand and that frequently they are difficult to separate. We frequently think of self-imposed demands as expectations that others have of us rather than what we ask of ourselves. As you read this discussion you may have noted that much of it seemed familiar. These demands were first discussed in Method 7, "Revise Unspoken Rules," and an effective way of reducing self-imposed demands is to discover the unspoken rule involved and to revise it.

Another self-imposed demand comes from the tendency to be some-one other than who we really are. Many people have an image of the type of person they feel they should be, and they reject the selves that they are. We're not talking about the natural and helpful desire to grow and improve but about the rejection that comes from lack of self-acceptance. You met this important topic in Method 2, "Recognize Stress As A Part Of Life," and you might want to review it not to see how lack of self-acceptance results in a number of self-imposed demands.

15G—CHOOSE BATTLES CAREFULLY

As we attempt to relate to others and make our way in the world, we will frequently encounter difficulties and frustrations. Often circumstances will not be as we wish: people will be unresponsive; frustrations will occur. We must decide when to take things as they are and when to fight to change them. That decision is a difficult one, and each person can decide in each situation which path to take. (Again, see Method 3.) We will be helped if we remember that struggles take considerable time and effort—they are stressful. We would do well to choose our battles carefully.

Some situations can't be changed very much. If I chose to protest every time Congress did something I didn't like, I'd write to Congress at least once a day. I save that energy by taking Congress as it is and writing only on matters that are of particular importance to me. When people around us have habits which are annoying, we can talk to them about our concerns, but we are foolish to make every concern a major issue. Save the energy for struggles which are important. Many people invite stress by confusing the unimportant with the important and continually fighting situations which might well be left alone.

Think of the areas in your life where you are working to get someone or something changed, particularly those that demand considerable energy and effort on your part. These are your battles. Consider whether it is possible to give up some of these battles. Select which are the important ones and decide to let the others go. Is it that necessary to fight each situation you don't like? Can you focus your energy on the few battles that will make a genuine difference for you and give up those that are insignificant? Perhaps your spouse has an annoying habit that you can decide to live with rather than criticize. Maybe your supervisor has a way of giving instructions that you don't like but can learn to tolerate. Consider carefully those battles which are important enough to take your time and energy and consciously say to yourself, "I need not fight the insignificant battles any longer." Exercise 6 at the end of this unit will help you choose your battles carefully.

EXERCISES

1. In column I below, list seven activities which take a significant portion of your time. Avoid overly large categories (work, school, family, etc.) and list specific activities in each category. In column II, estimate how many hours you devote to each task each week. In column III, put a number from 1 to 5 which indicates how willing you are to spend less time on that activity—or even to eliminate it altogether. The number 1 means not willing at all; 3 means moderately willing; 5 means very willing.

I. ACTIVITY   II. TIME SPENT   III. WILLINGNESS

_____

_____

_____

_____

_____

_____

Now take seven 3 × 5 cards and label them from A to G. Record each activity on a separate card. Take these cards two at a time and ask yourself, "Which of these is more important to me than the other?" When you decide, record a mark by the letter which is on the card listing that activity. Use the directions which follow to be sure that you compare all possible combinations. When you have finished, list the activities in the space provided, putting the activity with the most marks in position 1, the one with the second highest number of marks in position 2, and so on. This constitutes your priority list.

Procedure for comparisons: Compare the activity on card A with that on card B. Which is more important to you? If A, put a mark beside A in the "count column" below. If B, then put a mark beside B. Then continue this procedure with the following pairs: A-C, A-D, A-E, A-F, A-G, B-C, B-D, B-E, B-F, B-G, C-D, C-E, C-F, C-G, D-E, D-F, D-G, E-F, E-G, F-G.

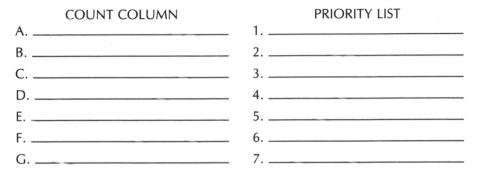

COUNT COLUMN	PRIORITY LIST
A. _____	1. _____
B. _____	2. _____
C. _____	3. _____
D. _____	4. _____
E. _____	5. _____
F. _____	6. _____
G. _____	7. _____

2. Prepare a plan for reducing demand. Beginning with the activity lowest on your list of priorities, ask yourself how you can spend less time on that activity. Do you need to spend as much time on that activity as you currently do? Is it as important as you have been assuming? Although you would prefer to spend more time on this activity, do you need to? Would there be disastrous consequences if you did not? Decide how you will spend less time on that activity—and on every activity as you move up your list of priorities. Record your plans below.

Plan for Reducing Demand

Ways to reduce demand No. 7 on priority list: _____

_____

_____

Ways to reduce demand No. 6 on priority list: _____

_____

_____

Ways to reduce demand No. 5 on priority list: _____

_____

_____

Ways to reduce demand No. 4 on priority list: _____

_____

_____

Ways to reduce demand No. 3 on priority list: _____

_____

_____

Ways to reduce demand No. 2 on priority list: _____

_____

_____

Ways to reduce demand No. 1 on priority list: _____

_____

_____

3. Select at least three situations involving your relationships with other people which are stressful for you. Describe each one in a few sentences. Think through each situation carefully to see if there is some demand that the other person is placing on you— some way that the other person wants you to be. Record that demand. Then ask yourself if you want to fulfill that demand, and if not, consciously and deliberately decide to refuse it.

Situation 1: _____

_____

_____

_____

Demand: _____

_____

_____

_____

Situation 2: _____

_____

_____

_____

Demand: _____

_____

_____

_____

Situation 3: _____
_____
_____
_____

Demand: _____
_____
_____
_____

4. Select at least three situations which are stressful for you, particularly situations in which you feel badly about yourself. Select
   situations in which you are angry at yourself, upset with yourself, ashamed, guilty, or concerned about your faults, limitations, or failures. Describe each one in a few sentences. Think
   through each one carefully to see if there is some demand that
   you are making on yourself—some internal expectation that you
   are expecting yourself to meet. Record that demand. Then ask
   yourself if you must fulfill that demand: Is it reasonable? Is it
   absolutely necessary? Would it be disastrous if you didn't fulfill
   it? When appropriate, consciously and deliberately decide to
   refuse that demand.

Situation 1: _____
_____
_____
_____

Demand: _____
_____
_____

Situation 2: _____
_____
_____

Demand: _____
_____
_____

Situation 3: _____
_____
_____
_____

Demand: _____

_____

_____

5.   Seat yourself comfortably in a chair, close your eyes, and im-
     agine yourself in one of the situations selected in Exercise 4.
     Fantasize about that situation for a few minutes, experiencing
     the situation as vividly as you can. Then repeat to yourself
     statements like the following:

     I am a human being and therefore imperfect.

     While I strive to improve myself, I also accept myself as I am.

     I won't feel badly about my human faults and weaknesses.

     The best thing I can do for myself right now is to accept myself
     as I am.

     Repeat this procedure for each situation in Exercise 4 and
record your reactions below.

Reactions to this exercise: _____

_____

_____

_____

_____

6.   Make a list of battles that you are currently fighting: people you
     quarrel with; situations you are protesting; arguments you are
     having. Put an X beside each battle which is genuinely impor-
     tant and worth the aggravation it costs you. Cross out all the
     others—conscientiously and deliberately decide not to fight
     them anymore.

CURRENT BATTLES	THIS BATTLE IS IMPORTANT
_____	
_____	_____
_____	_____
_____	_____
_____	_____
_____	_____
_____	_____
_____	_____
_____	_____

METHOD 16

ASSUME CONTROL

Have you ever been in a situation when you felt you had no control over what was happening to you? All of us have experienced such predicaments and know how uncomfortable we feel in them. A general rule of stress is this: The less control we exercise in any situation, the more stressful that situation is for us, other things being equal. People who feel that life is happening to them rather than that they are influencing what happens, undergo considerable stress. An older person who must enter a nursing home finds that experience more stressful if she feels that she is being forced into those living arrangements than if she were to make the move voluntarily. Talking about control with a musician once, I got this response, "I'm usually anxious before any concert, and yet I choose to perform publicly. How do you account for that?" Anxiety before each concert was understandable, but what would happen if she no longer genuinely desired to perform but was forced to in order to earn a living? How much more stressful that would be.

When vocational stress is discussed, people often point to the executive as the prototype of the heart-attack–ulcer–hypertension-prone individual. The demands and responsibilities of management are seen as a severe source of stress. In fact, although the executive does experience stress, indicators of vocational stress show that secretaries and assembly-line workers experience much more stress on the job than executives. Why? Because secretaries and assembly-line workers have much less control over their work day. They often must do what they are told to do and when they are told to do it. Often they can't set the order of their tasks, take rest breaks when they wish, or exercise control in ways which, though small, are significant in reducing stress. Executives may have heavy responsibilities and certainly aren't free to do as they please, but there are many times in their work day when they can exercise some free choice, and as a result, they experience less stress.

Much stress is experienced by the general population today because many people feel that they have less and less control over their lives. Government and big business seem to be making decisions that affect us daily and over which we believe we have little or no control. Ask parents how much control they have over children, particularly teens! Anything we can do for ourselves, for workers, and for the general public that increases control helps to reduce stress.

16A—ADOPT AN ATTITUDE OF RESPONSIBILITY

Do you often feel that life is happening *to* you and that you can't do much about it? Does the stress in your life seem to come from circumstances you have little or no control over? You will find your stress easier to manage if you begin to think of yourself as being more in control, and you can do this by reminding yourself of your share of the responsibility you have in the situation—no matter how small that responsibility may be. Look for choices you made that helped bring the situation about and choices you are making that keep the situation going. Even in situations that are 99 percent out of your hands, you can focus on the 1 percent control you have. It may not be much, but it helps. When you see yourself making choices and being at least partly responsible, you cease to feel like a victim. Even suffering, voluntarily assumed, is less burdensome than that which we perceive as inflicted on us.

See if you can find the choices you have made and the control you have exercised even in situations that seem totally out of your control. When someone makes a promise to you and then suddenly, willfully breaks it, you can at least recognize that you chose to trust that person. If a lover jilts you, you can acknowledge that you chose to love that person. If you have an unreasonable supervisor or co-worker, you can remind yourself each morning that you chose to continue to go to work there rather than look for another job or become unemployed.

Even when we consider ourselves not responsible for a situation, we can remind ourselves how responsible we are for our reaction to the situation. Our emotional response to something that happens to us results from the situation itself. Suppose that three people are criticized by their friends. The first considers this shameful and is depressed. The second sees this as an injustice and is angry. The third views it as a challenge and is invigorated. It wasn't the criticism that resulted in these feelings—it was the way that different people reacted that lead to different feelings.

We are responsible for how we feel. Instead of saying, "You made me angry," I can say, "I am angry at you—I make myself angry—because I don't like what you did." Rather than thinking that events make you depressed, remind yourself that you are depressed because you don't like what has happened, because you feel that things won't get better, and because you have a tendency to blame yourself. Whenever you find yourself experiencing a stressful emotion, remind yourself of your thoughts and beliefs that led to that emotion. Assume responsibility for your feelings instead of seeing them as being caused by other people or events beyond your control.

There are two dangers to be avoided in assuming an attitude of responsibility. First, when you see yourself as responsible, be careful not to assume all the responsibility: other people are responsible too. If someone lies to me, I can see myself as responsible in that I chose to believe that person, but that in no way alleviates the other person's responsibility for having lied. Few of us are totally responsible for any situation. You will feel better when you accept your share of the responsibility and insist that others accept theirs.

Second, do not confuse responsibility with blame. If the attitude of responsibility results in constantly blaming yourself whenever you are stressed, you won't be helping reduce that stress at all. With an attitude of responsibility, you can recognize the part you played in your own stress without blaming yourself for having done so. The self-accepting person can adopt an attitude of responsibility more easily than one who is overly self-critical. Consider the difference between blame and responsibility before trying to see yourself as more responsible.

16B—DO SOMETHING SPECIFIC

A while ago there was a very severe airplane crash in which the mutilated bodies of the victims were scattered over a wide area. Rescue workers on the scene found a horrible situation, and for weeks thereafter they showed the signs of stress that working there induced: sleeplessness, nightmares, tension, phobias. But one group of rescue workers showed fewer signs of stress than others: the policemen on the scene who arrested bystanders trying to loot souvenirs. Why? These police were able to do something specific and concrete in this situation. That resulted in a feeling of some control and less helplessness.

Any time you can engage in some specific activity in connection with your stress, you feel better. Never underestimate the powerful effect of some specific action on reducing stress, even in situations where we feel we have absolutely no control. Probably the strongest feelings of helplessness come as we learn that someone we love is dying of an incurable disease. This is the sort of situation we cannot control in any significant way, but by doing something specific we can ease our feelings of helplessness and powerlessness. What specific things can we do? We can help the dying person be as comfortable as possible. We can visit, read to him or her, and share time and conversation as often as possible. We can help him or her utilize the resources of a hospice. We can fight the disease by raising money for the organization that seeks its cure. We can do volunteer work in a hospital and thus become a part of our society's healing resources. Thus, even in the most hopeless of situations, there are concrete, specific things we can do to manage stress.

16C—SEEK INFORMATION

Knowledge is power! We feel more victimized by what we do not understand; the more we know about a given situation, the more we feel we have some control over it. Thus, in the example of experiencing the terminal illness of someone we love, we can, in addition to the suggestions already given, learn more about the disease. Then we will know more about what is happening and what to expect. This enables us to prepare ourselves for what is to come—and that is control.

The possibility of a tax audit is stressful for most people. What if the Internal Revenue Service (IRS) notified you that your tax return was to be audited? You could help deal with that situation by learning all you could about tax audits: what procedures are followed; what questions are asked; what rights you have; what happens if a deduction you have made is disallowed.

How often have you heard, "Everybody talks about the weather, but no one does anything about it"? Still, people who live in parts of the country subject to hurricanes and floods learn all they can about these natural phenomena and how to survive them. The more they learn, the more control they feel they have over their lives when these disasters hit.

16D—MAKE CHOICES AND DECISIONS

We feel more in control when we consciously make choices and decisions. Instead of making them so routinely that they are unnoticed, make a point of noting when you are making choices. People entering a hospital give up much of their autonomy, and everything that can be done to give them some choices, even small ones, helps to make their stay less stressful. Thus, even the opportunity for the patient to select dishes from a menu is helpful.

Since the death of someone we love evokes the greatest feelings of helplessness and powerlessness, let's look at that situation again. What choices can we make? In the past, funeral directors tried to help families by doing all the work and making all the decisions for them—or at least, as many as they could. Now clergy and funeral directors are increasingly offering opportunities for the bereaved to make as many choices as they (the bereaved) wish. In some faiths, people can choose to have certain passages read or certain hymns sung in the service. People can make choices about how to dress the deceased, visiting hours, open versus closed casket, and whether to be present when certain parts of the procedure (like the final closing of the casket) are conducted.

16E—BE ASSERTIVE

People who are unassertive experience much less control in their lives than people who are able to speak up for themselves and act on their own behalf. The submissive person is very much at the mercy of the wishes of other people. Thus, in addition to its benefits, assertiveness gives us more control in our lives and enables us to stop feeling victimized so frequently. Assertiveness has already been discussed in this guide (Method 10, "Develop Competencies") and now would be a good time to review the material discussed earlier.

EXERCISES

1. Think of a situation which is stressful for you. Describe this situation in a way which suggests that you have absolutely no control over it and that you have absolutely no responsibility for it.

   _____

   _____

   _____

   _____

   _____

   Now rethink this situation and try to see any choices you made to bring it about or any responsibility you may have for the situation. Think of anything you can do to affect this situation. Describe it as a situation for which you are responsible and over which you have control.

   _____

   _____

   _____

   _____

   _____

   What specific things can you do in this situation which might make it less stressful?

   _____

   _____

   _____

   What information might you seek in this situation which might make it less stressful?

   _____

   _____

   _____

   _____

What choices and decisions have you made, are you making, and could you make to affect this situation?

_____

_____

_____

_____

·   Why are you not doing those things which you can do to make this situation less stressful?

_____

_____

_____

_____

2.   Seat yourself comfortably in a chair, close your eyes, and imagine yourself in a stressful situation. Fantasize about that situation for a few minutes, experiencing it as vividly as you can. First, fantasize that the situation is out of your control and is one in which you can do nothing. Next, imagine that another person is in the situation and that she/he is actively doing things to handle it. Finally, imagine yourself as the strong, competent person who is in control of the situation and actively mastering it.

Reactions to this exercise:_____

_____

_____

_____

_____

3.   Think of situations or people that you believe make you angry, upset, depressed, jealous, etc. Think of what it is about those people or situations that cause you to feel as you do. Then change your thinking, assume responsibility for your feelings, and indicate why you make yourself feel as you do. The spaces below allow you to record your thinking in this exercise.

_____ makes me angry because _____

_____

In reality, I make myself angry because _____

_____

_____ upsets me because _____

_____

In reality, I make myself upset because _____

_____

_____ makes me depressed because _____

_____

In reality, I make myself depressed because _____

_____

_____ makes me jealous because _____

_____

In reality, I make myself jealous because _____

_____

_____ makes me anxious because _____

_____

In reality, I make myself anxious because _____

_____

METHOD 17

REDUCE UNCERTAINTY

We've all heard the statement, we fear the unknown—and in many ways that statement is quite true. We all tend to experience more stress when facing situations that we do not understand or that we know very little about. The more certain we are about what to expect in a given situation or what is expected of us, the more stress we experience. One way to manage stress, therefore, is to reduce uncertainty.

Take, for example, a person who has just learned that he has a disease and will need to be hospitalized for a period of time. That is certainly a stressful situation. Once a person hears that he is in such a situation, a host of questions comes to his mind: What is the disease like? What course will it take? Will it be painful? What effects will it have on me? How long will I be in the hospital? What will it be like there? What will all this cost me? Does my medical insurance cover it? The more that such questions are left unanswered, the greater the stress. The more answers there are—and the more complete the answers—the more the stress is reduced.

To take a less serious example, think of times when you have been invited out to a social event with a group of people you don't know. You might worry about what to wear, what these people like, what they talk about, and what interests them? When you enter an unfamiliar social situation where you don't know what to expect, you are much more apt to be worried than when you do know what to expect.

17A—SEEK INFORMATION

Some uncertainty results from lack of knowledge or information. Other uncertainty comes from unfamiliarity or from ambiguity. *Unfamiliarity* and *ambiguity* are quite similar—and we talk about them together—but these terms do have different meanings. If I am to have an operation and have never been in a hospital before, then I face an unfamiliar situation. When I have a job to do but am unclear about what is expected of me, that is an ambiguous situation. Since I may have done that job before, I may be familiar with it, and I may be familiar with the sense of ambiguity I feel when doing it! Thus, the three components of uncertainty are lack of information and knowledge, unfamiliarity, and ambiguity.

Here are some brief examples of stress-producing situations and of how that stress may be managed by increasing knowledge and information, reducing unfamiliarity, and resolving ambiguity. A young woman learns that she is pregnant for the first time. Her stress will be reduced if she learns as much as she can about pregnancy: the course it takes, its effects; how she will feel, what she can do (and avoid doing) to increase the health of her baby, what delivery is like, and many other areas. Similarly, the more she learns about how to care for an infant, the less she will worry about her coming duties as a mother.

A child's family that is moving into a new home in a different neighborhood. That child's stress can be reduced by visiting the new neighborhood in advance, meeting the children on her new block, visiting her new school, and learning about the reasons for the move and the process of the move itself.

In the previous unit (Method 16, "Assume Control") I used the example of a person who has been told that the Internal Revenue Service (IRS) wants to audit last year's return. A very useful step for him to take would be to find someone who has recently had a tax audit, then talk with that person to learn how it is conducted and what to expect. He can also read up on tax rules and regulations and talk with the IRS in advance about their procedures. Seeking information thus involves two methods of stress control: assume control and reduce uncertainty.

We could multiply examples by the hundred, but the principle is always the same: do all you can to gain information to reduce unfamiliarity and resolve ambiguity, and you will reduce the stress you experience. How do we accomplish this? Actively seek information about any situation you are in. Learn about what is coming. Ask questions—lots of them. Ask your teacher, your physician, your employer, your accountant, i.e., anyone involved with you, to tell you all they can. Read; explore; probe. Whenever you find yourself uncertain about something, find a way to eliminate that uncertainty. If your employer gives you directions that are unclear, ask for clarification. When you don't know what to expect, find out. The more you become familiar with a situation, the more you know what to expect, the clearer you are about expectations and directions, the more you take the mystery out of any situation, the less stress you will experience.

These efforts to learn all we can about a situation help us by reducing the uncertainty involved. They help us for other reasons as well. The more we know about a situation, the less we are going to be upset by false beliefs and myths. Considerable heartache, grief, guilt, and anxiety are caused by myths people hold about particular situations. The death of a child is probably the single most anguishing, stressful event that can happen to anyone. Often very young children die of no apparent cause. A child is put in its crib, left to go to sleep, and discovered dead a few hours later. This phenomena, known as *sudden infant death syndrome*, or crib death, is terrible in itself. But the tragedy is compounded when parents, ignorant of the facts, assume that they must have somehow caused the death. Perhaps they let the baby smother; maybe they fed it wrong; certainly they did something to shorten the baby's life. We don't understand crib death, but we do know that when it happens, it just happens, and nothing the parents did or did not do is responsible for it. Countless hours of anguished guilt could be eliminated if all parents understood that fact.

Knowledge about a situation can also give us the sense of confidence and assurance that comes from knowing that we understand it. Somehow we feel more in control or less victimized by what we understand. For example, a father learned that his teen-age son was killed in an auto accident. Nothing could eliminate his grief, of course. But as he went to the scene of the accident, learned all of the details of the accident, and understood exactly what happened, he felt a little better about it. He still grieved, but his grief was moderated by the realization that he knew and understood what happened to end his son's life.

17B—TAKE ACTION

We have been talking about seeking information as a way to reduce uncertainty. We can also become more familiar with certain situations by taking appropriate actions. Suppose, for example, you have to give a talk before a group of people, and the prospect of having to do this is stressful for you. This is a new situation for you; you are not familiar with it and feel uncomfortable about it. There are a number of things you can do to make the situation less strange for you. After you have the speech prepared, practice it wearing the same clothes you will wear when giving the speech. Have your notes prepared exactly the way you will use them— don't practice from handwritten notes and then type them up just before giving the talk. If at all possible, practice giving the talk in the room where it will be given or one as much like it as you can find. By doing these things, when you actually start to give the talk—wearing the same clothes and looking at the same notes—the situation won't be quite so strange for you and, accordingly, will be less stressful. Take any stressful task and see how you can practice it in advance to become familiar with it. The exercises for this unit help you apply the methods of seeking information and taking action appropriate to your stressful situations.

In general then, the more we learn about a situation, the more misinformation we eliminate from the situation, and the more action we can take to make a situation more familiar to us, the less stressful the situation will be. Of course, we are talking about situations that are stress producing: a new job, a move, a disease. Certainly there are times in your life where surprise or mystery are welcome. If someone invites you out to dinner for your birthday and says, "I want to surprise you and not tell you where we are going," that's not a time to reduce uncertainty—unless, of course, this was for some reason a stressful situation for you. As is always the case, the principle of reducing uncertainty applies to some situations and not to others—and you must use your own judgment. Further, there are times when no matter how hard we try, we cannot reduce uncertainty. At such times, we can help ourselves by tolerating the uncertainty that cannot be reduced (see Method 9, "Tolerate Uncertainty").

SPECIAL AREAS OF UNCERTAINTY

We want to reduce uncertainty in many situations we face. However, there are three types of situations which require special mention: human relationships, double messages, and role ambiguity.

Human Relationships

The most ambiguous stimuli of all are those found in our interactions with other people. Knowing what other people think or feel and determining what they want or expect can sometimes be extremely difficult. People often don't tell us directly what they think or want, either because they are reluctant to or because they don't know how. Thus, if we wonder what another person is thinking about us or whether a particular person cares for us, we may have a difficult time finding out. We can deal with this in a very simple way: ask. Ask another person what she thinks. Ask him how he feels. Ask them what they want. We won't always get an honest answer to our question, and sometimes we'll feel uncomfortable in trying. But often we will succeed. Taking the time to ask people simply and directly for information about their wants, needs, and feelings will help us considerably.

Double Messages

Often we have difficulty communicating with other people because they send us double messages. Thus, a person tells you he loves you one day and then acts as though he was indifferent to you the next day. The book *Stop! You're Driving Me Crazy* by Bach and Deutsch deals extensively with this problem, citing examples of people being soliticious of us on one occasion but forgetting what is important to us on other occasions. Sometimes a person will say to us, "I don't care what we do tonight," and then gives indications that he really does care. The uncertainty created by these double messages is dealt with in the same way as in other human relationships. Ask the other person what he or she really wants. Explain that you are uncertain about their wishes and ask for clarification. You won't always get it—but it's always worth a try.

Role Ambiguity

We expect different types and categories of people to behave in certain ways. We expect leaders to make decisions and assume responsibility. We expect doctors to be knowledgeable and helpful. We expect children to prefer play to study. The behaviors we expect from people in certain positions in life are role behaviors. Recently, the typical role behaviors expected of men and women have been challenged. Our ideas of what it means to be male and female have been changing rapidly, and as a result our ideas of how men and women should relate to each other have also changed. In this period of change, different people have different ideas on behavior, and there is no consensus. Thus, people often find themselves uncertain about what behavior is expected of them, what is approved of or disapproved of, and what reactions they might get from others. This is particularly true of women at work where the more they adopt role behaviors appropriate to their new positions, the more others may see them as unfeminine.

This role ambiguity is a difficult problem and there is no simple answer to it. We can deal with stress resulting from this ambiguity by accepting the fact that the ambiguity exists, recognizing that there is no one right answer to the problem at the moment, and seeking clarification whenever possible. We can sit down with our friends and colleagues, talk it over, and work out a way to reduce some of the uncertainty.

EXERCISES

1. Below are a number of situations which many people would find stressful. In the space provided, list ways in which uncertainty and unfamiliarity could be reduced in each situation. Remember that the three components of uncertainty are lack of information and knowledge, unfamiliarity, and ambiguity.

    Job hunting:_____

    _____

    _____

    _____

Trip to a strange city:_____

_____

_____

_____

Divorce:_____

_____

_____

_____

Entering college:_____

_____

_____

_____

Investing money:_____

_____

_____

_____

A stressful situation you currently face:_____

_____

_____

_____

Another stressful situation you currently face:_____

_____

_____

_____

2. Space is provided below for you to record the names of five people who are important in your life. Think about your relationships with those people: what questions do you have about the relationship which are unanswered? In what ways are you uncertain about how the other person thinks or feels? What about the reactions of that person or your relationship to that person do you find confusing or unclear? What double messages do you believe the other person is sending? Record these areas of uncertainty in each relationship in the space provided, and then think about and record how you will go about reducing that uncertainty.

Person:_____ Areas of uncertainty:_____

_____

_____

_____

_____

Ways to reduce uncertainty:_____

_____

_____

_____

_____

Person:_____ Areas of uncertainty:_____

_____

_____

_____

_____

Ways to reduce uncertainty:_____

_____

_____

_____

_____

Person:_____ Areas of uncertainty:_____

_____

_____

_____

_____

Ways to reduce uncertainty:_____

_____

_____

_____

_____

Person:_____ Areas of uncertainty:_____

_____

_____

_____

_____

Ways to reduce uncertainty:_____

_____

_____

_____

_____

Person:_____ Areas of uncertainty:_____

_____

_____

_____

_____

Ways to reduce uncertainty:_____

_____

_____

_____

_____

METHOD 18

FINISH UNFINISHED BUSINESS

All of us know how it feels when we have a lot of work that is unfinished, particularly when there is a deadline by which the work must be completed. The work is on your mind, eating away at you, and interfering with your attempts to relax, rest, or work on other business. You are apt to keep thinking about it and reminding yourself that the work is still incomplete. Unfinished business can create tension; sometimes we can't quite rest completely until it is done. Like the tension created by hearing one shoe drop, tension from unfinished business can stay with us until we finish it completely. Of course, the tension created by unfinished business is not necessarily great, nor does it always result in considerable stress. But even the little tensions can add up, and when you have a lot of unfinished business, your stress level is increased. Whenever we can reduce the amount of unfinished business in our lives, we reduce stress.

Our unfinished business consists of more than just specific tasks that need to be completed. A second type of unfinished business that we must examine is the unfinished business in our emotional lives: emotions that have not been expressed and interpersonal relationships. Think of a time when you were in a situation that made you angry, but you did not express that anger. Perhaps you are reluctant to express anger at any time or perhaps that particular moment seemed inappropriate for such expression. Whatever the reason, you buried that anger. Most students of human behavior agree that the anger doesn't go away. When you bury it, unexpressed, it stays with you, even without your being aware of it, and can be experienced as added tension in your life. Unexpressed anger is unfinished business. The way to rid yourself of that tension and its resulting stress is to express your anger.

Another emotion that we often suppress is grief. When we experience a serious loss, such as the death of someone we love, the loss of a job or promotion, or any other major loss, we must work through the long, complicated process called *grief*. Unfortunately, we are often so reluctant to show our emotions or to experience the pain of grief that we do not permit ourselves to complete the process. Strangely, we praise people for bearing their burdens quietly and stoically rather than encourage them to cry, feel their sorrow, and let the grief process heal them. Unexpressed grief, like hidden anger, stays with us and takes its toll until we express it.

While grief and anger are the two prime examples of unexpressed emotion, the same principles apply to any emotions that are suppressed rather than expressed: unexpressed emotions are unfinished business.

The third type of unfinished business stems from personal relationships that lack completion or closure. Suppose you learn that a friend of yours believes something about you that is untrue. You want to meet and talk with him so that you can explain the error and present the truth as you see it. Until you experience the sense of completion that comes with that explanation, you have unfinished business. Another friend moves away suddenly, and you realize that there were many things you wanted to say to him but didn't—that's unfinished business. Still another friend has said some things that make you confused about what she really thinks of you. Until you clear up that confusion, you have more unfinished business.

A fourth kind of unfinished business consists of decisions that need to be made. Whenever you have to make a decision, even a minor one, you must expend effort, and that results in some stress. Considerably more stress comes when we worry and fret over decisions, postpone them, and let them prey on our minds. As the number of these unmade decisions increases, stress increases. Unmade decisions are unfinished business.

Thus, unfinished business consists of tasks needing completion, emotions needing expression, personal relationships needing closure, and decisions to be made. As you review unfinished business in your own life, you may find it difficult to distinguish among these four types and find that a particular situation may involve two or three of them. The four types are very much like each other, and you need not be concerned about deciding which type of unfinished business a given situation represents. Instead, spend your time finishing that unfinished business, using one of the methods discussed below.

18A—COMPLETE TASKS

The most obvious way to deal with unfinished business is to finish it! Just do it. Clear your desk of incompleted work. Although the problem of unfinished business is more complicated than that, don't overlook the fact that often we let little things pile up until they become an irritant. When you find yourself using energy worrying about all the things that aren't finished, make a list of them and set out to accomplish them one by one. Be sure to check off each item as it is completed so that you can watch your progress. Most of us have a few chores that we would rather not have to do. We keep procrastinating, thinking that we'll do them tomorrow, and eventually spend more time and energy worrying about them than it would take to complete them.

18B—SET SHORT-TERM GOALS

Some major tasks cannot be completed quickly. A student writing a major term paper cannot complete it in one week. An executive who is working on a long-range plan cannot rush its completion. An author cannot finish a book the week it's begun. Some tasks are never completed no matter how much we work at them. I want to keep up in my field, but there is no end to the number of books and articles I could read. A manager is always thinking and planning—business does not stand still. You can deal with situations such as these by setting reasonable short-term goals. As you reach each goal, you can have the sense of completion that comes from knowing that you have accomplished something specific. This sense of completion replaces the constant uneasiness that comes from thinking that you are never getting anywhere. By taking careful note of what you have done, you reduce the stress that comes from focusing on what you have not done.

Thus, a person writing a long report can break it into units and take note of each unit as it is completed. A student can decide to accomplish so many pages in the text each week or spend so many hours each week and note her progress as time passes. Setting and completing short-term goals, particularly when our task is very large or even never-ending, effectively lessens our tension as we see ourselves accomplishing something. It also reduces the complexity of our task (see Method 15C, "Make Activities Less Complex").

18C—ESTABLISH RESERVED TIME

Some of our unfinished business consists of worrying about problems that must be solved and decisions that must be made. We find ourselves worrying or fretting about them all the time. When this begins to be a problem, reserve some specific time for dealing with it. Suppose you set aside Tuesday night from 8 to 10 p.m. as your reserved time. At any other time during the week when the problems or decisions begin to prey on your mind, you can say to yourself, "I've already planned to work on this Tuesday night—I need not concern myself with it now." The realization that you have set aside time for thinking through the problem or making the decision will make it easier for you to let it go at other times. It's like saying, "I'll worry about this tomorrow," with the confidence that you are not just procrastinating.

18D—MAKE DECISIONS

Like the advice to complete tasks, the suggestion that you make decisions seems obvious. But if you look at the stress you have experienced in the past, you may find that much tension results from fretting about and even obsessing about some decisions that just need to be made. There are two major reasons for continually postponing decisions: (1) we are afraid to risk making a wrong decision; (2) we know what the decision must be, but we don't like it and therefore keep ourselves from facing it. The recognition that risks must be taken and that decisions must be made without absolute certainty as well as knowing that unpleasant realities must be faced will help us make decisions. Remember that the risk you run by not making a decision may be greater than that involved in the decision itself. Similarly the unpleasant reality you are avoiding may well not be as bad as the unpleasantness that comes from avoiding it.

18E—EXPRESS YOUR EMOTIONS

The only effective way to deal with the tension coming from unexpressed emotions is to allow yourself full expression of those emotions. Gestalt psychologists, in particular, emphasize that everything you can do or learn that helps you have fuller emotional expression will lessen your stress. Learning to express your anger and allowing yourself to feel your grief would be a good start. If you have some things to say to someone, say them. Have it out with them. Another means for encouraging full expression is the empty chair technique, which you read about earlier in this guide (see Method 1, "Take Inventory"). If you are unable to express your feelings to someone in person, pretend they are with you by mentally placing them in an empty chair. Then talk to them, say whatever you have to say with as few reservations and inhibitions as you can. Yell, cry—experience emotions. If you've never done this before, you may feel a little awkward at first, but stick with it. It works!

Many people have such difficulty in expressing their feelings that they need more extensive help than this guide can provide. Securing training in assertiveness, reading more widely in the area, or seeking professional help are other actions which may be of assistance.

18F—WRITE IT OUT

Many people find that they can best release their emotions through writing. A daily diary or journal in which a person records, not the routine happenings of the day, but their feelings and reactions about those events is one form of such release. If you are very angry at a person, writing that person a long letter expressing your feelings might prove useful—even if you tear the letter up later and never send it. You can even write yourself a letter when you are angry at yourself. Talking with someone who has died by means of a written statement (as though you were going to send it to that person) can help handle your grief. Anytime you have a stressful emotion, writing your thoughts and feelings in a diary, letter, or any form you wish may be helpful. The only way you can learn if this approach is good for you is to try it.

18G—SEEK CLOSURE IN PERSONAL RELATIONSHIPS

When your relationship with someone seems incomplete because of confusion, ambiguities, misunderstandings, or unanswered questions, seek to clarify the situation. It's so simple—yet sometimes so difficult. If someone has a wrong impression of you, sit down with him and discuss the situation. When questions are unanswered, ask for clarification. If you are concerned about whether your friend or spouse or colleague understands you, talk to that person about it. Anytime you find yourself wondering, "I wonder what he is thinking" or "I wish I could say this to her," set out to have a good talk with that person. Seeking closure, like expressing emotions, can be a major problem for some people and may require resources beyond this guide.

Frequently a great deal of unfinished business accumulates because a person just never gets around to doing what is necessary to complete business. He or she may find expressing emotions, seeking closure, or making decisions difficult. The exercises for this unit help you get started and give you practice in finishing your unfinished business.

EXERCISES

1. Make a list of things that you have to do, i.e., jobs that need finishing. Put an X after each one which you believe is not completed largely because you have been putting it off. Reviewing those you have marked with an X, decide which one you will do first and put a 1 by it after the X: put a 2 by the one you will do second and a 3 by the one you will do third, etc., until you have completed the list.

   _____   _____

   _____   _____

   _____   _____

   _____   _____

   _____   _____

2. Looking again at the items in your list above, decide by when each of the marked jobs will be done and record the date by each item.

3. Select a large task or project that you must complete. Break it down into several parts, units, or stages; think of it not as one large project but as a series of smaller projects. Decide how long it will take to complete each of the parts and then set a goal for the completion of each part. Record this information in the space below.

Project needing completion:_____

_____

_____

Parts/Units/Stages	Time Needed	Goal (Date of Completion)
_____	_____	_____
_____	_____	_____
_____	_____	_____
_____	_____	_____
_____	_____	_____

4. Select a period of time from one-half hour to two hours which you can devote each week to thinking about your unfinished business. This is your reserved time. It should be a time when you know you will be free to think about unfinished business— or even to complete some of it. Record the time below.

Reserved time: Day _____ Hours _____

5. In the spaces below, list important decisions that you have to make. Select a date as your goal for making each decision and record that date in the proper space.

Decision	Date of Decision
_____	_____
_____	_____
_____	_____
_____	_____
_____	_____

6. Choose an emotion which you believe you have not been expressing fully: anger, anxiety, grief, etc. Then, depending on the circumstances and your wishes, select one of the following methods for helping you express that emotion more fully:
   a. Talk about the situation or person about which you have these feelings with a sympathetic listener. Ask your listen-

er to do nothing but listen carefully and provide some support. Advise him/her that you may become emotional during the discussion and to permit you that freedom.

b. Imagine that the person about whom you have these feelings is with you, sitting in an empty chair across from you. Talk to that person; without censuring yourself, say whatever comes to mind. Don't hold back. When you begin, you may be very unemotional. Keep at it long enough for the emotions to come. Then let yourself experience the emotions fully.

c. Go to the person about whom you have these feelings and ask for the opportunity to discuss the situation over with him/her. Explain how you feel and let your emotions come. In short, "have it out" with that person. Obviously, you must use careful judgment in deciding when to use this method.

d. Write a letter to that person. Since you will not mail it, be as frank as you can be. Let your thoughts and feelings flow and say anything that is on your mind.

Reactions to this exercise:_____

_____

_____

_____

_____

_____

_____

METHOD 19

MINIMIZE CHANGE

There are times when a change of scenery is welcomed. As noted in the section on getting away from it all (Method 6), seeking a change in the way we do things or the place we spend our time now and then helps in the reduction of stress. It is also true, however, that too much or too rapid change can cause stress. Every time we experience a change, we must make an adjustment. Change often requires us to engage in different behaviors, learn new skills, or think in different ways. Although each of these adjustments may enrich our lives in the long run, too many of them at once are stressful.

We live in a rapidly changing world. Gone are the days when the average person is born, grows up, marries, works, and dies in the same town. People frequently change careers once, twice, and even more times. The social changes in the 1960s and 1970s, especially the sexual revolution and changing conceptions of male-female relationships, confronted all of us with challenging ideas and changing habits. Anyone in the business world knows of the ups and downs of the economy and the market. The energy crisis, concerns about the environment, and the Viet Nam experience forced many Americans to change their beliefs about the inevitability of progress and the ability of technology and power to solve all of our problems and get us whatever we want. The rate of change is increasing. Learning to live with and deal with change is a major problem for our generation.

While experiencing personal stress, we will want to minimize change. The more stability and certainty we can produce by minimizing change, the more we reduce stress. Minimizing change results in greater feelings of security and lessens our adjustive demand. This is especially true in periods of great personal upheaval. Minimizing change at such times is of great benefit.

How do we minimize change? Although there are a few general rules, each situation requires its own answer to this question. Let's take some illustrations. A married couple discovers that the wife's mother is now growing quite old and can no longer live by herself. They decide to invite her to live with them. This helpful move certainly involves changes for the older woman and thus is stressful. One way to minimize the change would be to clear out the guest room in the house and furnish it with the mother's personal furniture. In this way, even in a new home, she would be surrounded by the familiar and be in surroundings which she found comfortable. In the case of a young child, the stress of moving can be lessened in the same way. Pack the child's room carefully and then set it up in the new house to resemble the old room as much as possible. If you are planning new furniture for the child, wait a while. Wait until the child accommodates to the change of moving before introducing further change.

Moving is stressful for adults too. In a workshop involving many executives, men and women talked about the stress of moving from one community to another as the needs of the corporation changed. One executive told of how comforting it felt to him to attend church in the new community. When he entered the church of his faith, he saw familiar symbols, used a hymnal that he was used to, and in other ways found himself in a comforting situation. Those who belong to service organizations and analogous groups find them quite similar from community to community and that attending meetings of these groups in one's new town helps them cope with change. Certainly, for the refugees who fled Castro, the stress of moving out of Cuba was helped when these people found other Cubans in the United States and could eat Cuban food and sip cafe cubano.

When we experience a severe personal loss, such as the death of someone we love, a divorce, or some other separation, we can help ourselves by making as few other changes as possible while we adjust to our loss. A widow who feels that she should sell her home after the death of her husband may want to wait several months if possible, so that she need not deal with the loss of her husband and the loss of her home at the same time. She will also want to keep old friends and old habits, especially in the first months of mourning. People who retire or who become divorced and then make other major changes in their lives at the same time (e.g., moving to a new home, making a new circle of friends) are compounding the stress in an already stressful situation. We must recognize, of course, that avoiding such additional changes is often impossible; nevertheless, we should always do so when we can.

We should also attempt to schedule our changes whenever possible. People who practice family planning benefit if the births of children don't come too close to a major move, a new job, or a promotion. Women who decide to enter the work force for the first time can schedule other major changes in their lives for times other than their first week of work.

One way to help minimize change is to develop a daily routine that you can follow under all or almost all circumstances. If when you get up in the morning you have breakfast and then read the newspaper, doing that every day provides a stability on days when everything else is changing. Children seek this out when they go through a bedtime ritual of taking a bath, brushing their teeth, and then having a story told or read to them. Notice how sometimes they insist on the same story, over and over, word for word. They are making a secure and predictable world for themselves for at least part of the day! You can do the same. Anyone can develop a bedtime routine, early morning routine, or a routine for other parts of the day that can provide some stability in a changing world. A daily routine also has another benefit: it is one of the ways of taking care of yourself (Method 6F).

The exercises for this unit guide you in thinking about ways to minimize change in your life. In addition, remember that if we anticipate change, we will be in a better position to deal with it. Thus, the material on anticipating change is useful when you are thinking about minimizing change (see Method 10, "Anticipate Change").

All methods in this guide are more useful in some circumstances than in others. This is particularly true of minimizing change. At times, minimizing change is one of the most helpful steps you can take; at other times, you might want to seek change. As always, you need to examine each situation to decide which approach is best. A general principle is, The more a person is undergoing a period of personal distress and rapid change, the more one should try to minimize the change, avoid additional changes, and introduce periods of stability and familiarity. On the other hand, the more a person continues in a stressful routine or situation, the more one needs some change as a relief.

EXERCISES

1. Devise three one-half-hour routines which you could use daily in times of stress. Each routine should consist of activities which you enjoy or which at least are calming. One routine is for early morning, another is for the late afternoon, and the last is for late evening just before going to bed. Think of some activity or series of activities that you could engage in daily that would provide you with a comfortable, calm half hour that you could look forward to each day.

Early morning routine:_____

_____

_____

_____

Late afternoon routine:_____

_____

_____

_____

Late evening routine:_____

_____

_____

_____

2. Below are listed several situations that involve change (and places for you to list additional ones). In the space provided, indicate what might be done to minimize the change in each instance. In the spaces provided for other situations, list those which you are currently involved in or anticipate facing in the future.

Moving to a new town:_____

_____

_____

_____

Starting a new job:_____

_____

_____

_____

Moving to a new home:_____

_____

_____

_____

Other:_____

_____

_____

_____

Other:_____

_____

_____

_____

PART IV

WORKING ON THE ENVIRONMENT

One major way of controlling stress in our lives is to seek support by sharing our experiences and feelings with others and utilizing resources that are available to us. Experts in human behavior frequently disagree on definitions of stress and in their theories about stress, but there is no disagreement about the importance of support. Unfortunately, there will be times when we face a difficult period in our lives about which we can do very little and when even working on our attitudes and approaches to the problem are of little help. At such times we can use the methods described in Part IV to seek support. Remember, however, support is always important and should not be reserved only for those times when other methods fail. Seeking support should be a part of any stress management program.

METHOD 20

SEEK SUPPORT

A major source of help in times of stress is support. Anyone experiencing stress needs to seek out and utilize all possible sources of support. In this guide, *support* means (1) knowing that someone cares for you, understands you, and is there to help you and (2) obtaining information and assistance from other people and organizations.

Gaining support is knowing that someone is on your side, that you are not alone. Unfortunately, people who experience stress often suffer in silence. They don't tell others about their fears, anxieties, guilt, or stress, and this silence only makes their troubles worse. You are not alone in this world, and when you realize that fully, that realization in itself can help you manage stress.

How do we obtain support? There are six basic methods for obtaining and utilizing support in times of stress.

20A—TALK IT OUT

The first of these methods is very simple: share your stress with others. Talk about it. Tell others how you feel. Don't keep it to yourself.

When I was pastor of a church as a young man, I learned how important and helpful it is to share your stress with others. When someone in the parish died, I would make a pastoral call to the family and would often leave the home feeling bad—and even guilty. As a young, inexperienced pastor, I just didn't know what to say. I presumed that I should say something profoundly comforting or profoundly theological and I couldn't find those profound thoughts. I always felt that no matter what I said or did, it was inadequate.

How wrong I was! Often, a while after the funeral, friends of the family would tell me that members of the family had told them I had been a great help. Family members might have thanked me personally out of politeness, but when they told their friends they had received help, they must have meant it. I received considerable feedback about how helpful and comforting I had been.

Perhaps you have had such an experience. You listened to someone who was grieving, or experiencing some other stress, and felt you did nothing much to help but were thanked anyway. Or perhaps you have been in the other position—that of receiving the help. You were upset about something, and you talked it out with another person. And you felt better. You may not even remember what the other person said. The important thing was that someone was there.

We obtain support, then, by talking and sharing with other people. When you experience stress, seek out people with whom you can share your feelings. This does not mean always talking about yourself and dominating every conversation with your troubles. It means seeking appropriate opportunities and engaging in appropriate sharing.

Time and time again people tell me that they had gone through a difficult period of their lives but had told no one about it. They usually talk about not wanting to burden anyone. Sometimes we even make a virtue of silence saying, "How wonderful he is; he never lets anyone know about his difficulties." We tend to think of this silence as a strength and of sharing as weakness. At other times, we feel that others don't care or aren't interested. The suspicious among us believe that others will enjoy knowing we're in difficulty or will use that fact against us in some way.

The truth is, silence in times of difficulty is not golden—it is destructive. Some people may not be helpful, but most will be. We need not be afraid to share who we are. We will delight in the discovery that we are not alone.

Sharing your stress with anyone is helpful. Sharing it with someone you care for and respect is more helpful. Most helpful of all is sharing with someone who has experienced or is experiencing the same type of stress as you. A recent television program told of a telephone network for children suffering from terminal cancer. These children could make long-distance calls to other children in similar difficulty and just talk. They didn't always talk about their illness. They talked about things any child would talk about. But that sharing and that support did wonders for the children.

There are many examples of people finding support by sharing with others having similar difficulties. In many high schools, children of divorced parents meet periodically to talk about their experiences. Alcoholics Anonymous was founded on the principle of one alcoholic helping another. Now we have Al-Anon and Al-Ateen to bring families of alcoholics together for mutual support. The number of "anonymous" groups is growing: Gamblers Anonymous, Parents Anonymous (for child abusers), Neurotics Anonymous, and many more.

People about to retire will benefit from talking with those who are also about to retire (and those who have successfully retired). A young executive seeking a new position will benefit from talking with someone who has been through the job-hunting route before. A woman with a mastectomy will gain enormous help from talking to someone who has had the same operation. Regardless of your particular situation, you will find help by talking it over and sharing it with other people, particularly with someone who is going through or who has gone through the same difficulty.

This sharing helps for a number of reasons. It lets us know that we are not alone. The very fact that someone takes the time to listen to us tells us that we are cared for and valued. It makes a great difference to know you are not alone. In fact, knowing that there is someone we can talk with if we wish is comforting, even if we don't talk with them very much. Just knowing they are there may be enough.

Talking it out gets it off your chest. After talking for a while, you feel as though you have put down a great burden. Have you ever experienced grief or anger and, after talking it over with someone, found that the grief or anger was lessened? That's the release that comes with support. Many times people who tell me about their situation begin by talking quite rapidly in a tense voice. I've learned to remain relatively quiet and let them continue. After a while, once they feel safe and know that they are with someone who cares, they burst into tears. All the anguish that has been building up inside comes out. They have a good cry, and they feel better. Feelings that do not find some expression build up inside us and create all kinds of havoc (see Method 18, "Finish Unfinished Business"). The release gained through support is not only comforting, but also helps prevent further difficulties from developing.

Another benefit from sharing is a broadened perspective. When we talk out our problems with others, we understand them better—we see them in a different light. All too often, frustrations, angers, and disappointments that are not shared fester within us, and soon we lose all sense of proportion and perspective. A problem that I keep to myself is frequently distorted and looks worse than it is. When I share it with another person, I see it better myself.

Such perspective is gained by the very process of talking with another, regardless of what the other person says in return. But the other person's reaction can give us a further benefit, namely, feedback. The other person can respond to us and help us understand ourselves better. The most common benefit of this feedback is the realization that other people are not shocked or upset by our difficulties. A frequently overlooked fact is that people often feel guilty or awkward about their difficulties. Some people, for example, are ashamed of their fears. I think of the man who was afraid of heights but wouldn't tell anyone about it. For others, their own anger causes shame and guilt. And others believe that their family and friends would reject them if they shared their own feelings. All too frequently, people believe that their particular difficulty is strange or peculiar. Many times a person has said to me, "I'm probably the most messed-up person you've ever met," and then proceeded to tell me about a difficulty or feeling I've encountered many times before.

When we finally get our courage to tell a friend our fear or sense of inadequacy, and our friend doesn't express horror or laugh at us, but instead shows some understanding, our relief is enormous. There is no substitute for it. Such feedback from others helps remove our feelings of being strange, weird, or unworthy—and that certainly reduces stress.

Remember that we are talking only about the process of sharing our stress with others. We are not assuming that the other person can offer any specific help or advice or answers. (We'll come to that next.) We benefit from the process of sharing itself. Our problems are not solved, but we feel better and are better able to manage our stress.

20B—SEEK ADVICE AND COUNSEL

We have noted that talking it out involves sharing with another person without expecting much in return. But there are times when asking for specific advice and counsel is appropriate and useful. What do you do when you face a problem? If you always or most always try to solve problems all alone, you will find it helpful to learn to ask others for their help. A mother whose child seems unduly afraid of starting school might want to ask other mothers or teachers for advice on how to handle the situation. A person wondering whether to buy another house can ask a friend for advice. Seeking advice is obviously quite simple, but surprisingly many people fail to do it.

We can get considerable advice from friends and family. Talking with them and hearing what they have to say may help us. At times we need to seek expert advice. Few people would want to make a will without consulting a lawyer or invest a large amount of money without talking with an investment counselor or other financial advisor. People with personal difficulties beyond the scope of this guide will want to consider professional counseling or therapy when warranted.

20C—UTILIZE RESOURCES

We not only have other people to help us, we also have a world of resources. The person who knows how to locate and utilize resources has a much easier time of handling difficulties and managing stress. *Resources* here refers to publications and organizations that can give us information and advice on coping with stress. There is an abundance of resources for you to utilize, much of it free or very low cost, and you need to know how to tap those resources.

A person who is thinking about retiring must begin planning but might have a number of fears and a wide range of questions. In addition to talking it out with others and seeking advice and counsel, she can also tap a number of resources. Several national and regional organizations are devoted to the problems of retirement: she can write to and join one or more of them. Magazines, journals, newsletters, and radio and television programs deal with issues of retirement and aging. Many books have been written on the subject, as well as on special areas within retirement, such as nutrition or exercise for the older person. Some companies sponsor special workshops for people planning retirement. The U.S. Government Printing Office has a number of relevant publications. Insurance companies and financial institutions frequently issue materials devoted to financial planning and retirement. Most local governments will provide a list of organizations and agencies available for retired people. Moreover, each of these organizations and agencies has additional resources. When you consider how much help is available, it's amazing how many people approach retirement by planning for it all alone.

Retirement is only one area where resources are abundant. Resources are available to you for almost any stressful situation you encounter. When young people talk to me about career planning, I remind them that almost all occupational groups have a national organization and that by writing to that organization they can obtain valuable information. Women seeking to change the pattern of their lives can join women's groups. The Welcome Wagon assists people moving into a new town. Religious people find abundant help through membership in a church or synagogue. Adult education programs provide assistance on just about every area of living. Lily Tomlin used to say, "One way to help the needy is to give them what they need." Society has certainly found ways to give us what we need when facing stressful circumstances.

How can you locate and utilize these resources? Start with the local library. Librarians are very helpful people. They have access to worlds of information and are eager to share it with you. The librarian can direct you to books, pamphlets, and periodicals on subjects of interest to you and also show you directories of agencies and organizations that might help. Be sure to write to those organizations. Check with government agencies: local, county, state, and federal. In particular, don't forget the U.S. Government Printing Office. Don't be afraid to write to large companies, radio and television stations, newspapers and magazines, and book publishers to ask for help. (The library can help you find addresses). Use your own ingenuity; there are more resources out there than you think.

20D—CREATE SUPPORT SYSTEMS WHERE THEY DON'T EXIST

When you can't locate support or resources for your particular area of difficulty, maybe you can create a new support system. That's what the two founders of Alcoholics Anonymous did.

Today organizations for widows exist in many places. But if you are widowed and can't find one near you, try establishing one. People in financial stress often organize food co-ops or other cooperative buying programs. Establishing a new organization isn't easy, but it may be much more feasible than you think. And, by creating a new support system, you help others as well as yourself.

20E—PARTICIPATE IN RITUAL

Participation in ritual and ceremony is a source of considerable support. It is no surprise that societies establish rituals for most crucial (and therefore stressful) moments in life. Retirement parties, graduation ceremonies, weddings, funerals, and more informal ceremonies help by bringing us into contact with others, providing us with guides on how to react, and helping us share the experience and wisdom of others. Actually, the psychology of ritual and ceremony is a somewhat complicated area. Let it suffice here to note that participation in such ritual can be helpful in times of stress.

20F—SHARE IN OTHERS' EXPERIENCES

We can gain much strength and comfort in times of stress by learning that other people have had difficulties similar to ours and have successfully overcome them. Seeing how other people manage their stress gives us ideas for handling our own. Knowing that other people have had some of the same concerns as we do helps eliminate the feeling that we are somehow strange or different. The book *Passages* by Gail Sheehy, which received enormous attention from the general public, made its main contributions by informing readers that the crises they faced as they grew older were not unique. I spoke with many people after they had read the book, and I heard over and over again, "I never knew that other people went through this." Television may certainly be criticized for the quality of its productions, but still, shows such as "One Day at a Time" or "All in the Family" gives us the feeling that others share our struggles.

We can share others' experiences by reading or by viewing movies and television. We can also share in others' experiences by talking with them and listening to them. It helps not only to tell others about our stress but also to listen to others talk about theirs.

How do we begin seeking more support? Most ways of seeking support are quite easy and you can use them almost immediately. Many people, however, find that seeking support is easier when they review their stress and sources of support carefully. The exercises for this unit help you complete this review systematically.

EXERCISES

1. In the left-hand column of the chart below, using a few key words, list situations, worries, or concerns which are stressful for you. In the top row of the chart, name people with whom you come in contact regularly. Then place an X beside each stressful item under the name of each person with whom you have talked about your feelings on the item. When you have done this, the remaining empty spaces represent an opportunity for further seeking of support. Select a number of these opportunities (at least one of every four) and put a 0 in those spaces. In the next week, if possible, discuss the items listed with the people indicated by the spaces containing a 0.

PEOPLE

STRESSFUL ITEM	1.	2.	3.	4.	5.
1.					
2.					
3.					
4.					
5.					
6.					
7.					
8.					
9.					
10.					
11.					

2. In the space provided, list, using a few key words, problems that are now of concern to you. These may include some of the items used in Exercise 1. After each problem, state at least one person

to whom you can go for advice and counsel on this problem. Then, in the last column, indicate the date by which you promise yourself you will seek that advice and counsel from the person indicated.

PROBLEM	RESOURCE PERSON	DATE
_____	_____	_____
_____	_____	_____
_____	_____	_____
_____	_____	_____
_____	_____	_____
_____	_____	_____
_____	_____	_____

3. Take three problems which are of concern to you and which you believe might be better handled if you had more information. Go to your local library and find out what materials exist—books, periodicals, government publications, etc. Ask the librarian to help you. Develop a list of other resources as well. Then use the materials and resources to help you with your problems.

Problem 1: _____

_____

_____

_____

Materials and other resources: _____

_____

_____

_____

_____

Problem 2: _____

_____

_____

_____

Materials and other resources: _____

_____

_____

_____

_____

Problem 3: _____

_____

_____

Materials and other resources: _____

_____

_____

_____

_____

PART V

APPLYING THE METHODS

You have now learned each of the twenty basic methods for coping with stress. If these methods are to become a part of your daily thinking as you face stressful situations, you need to practice using them. The exercises which accompany each method give you some practice in using the methods; Part V of this book gives you another kind of practice. Now you have the opportunity to read accounts of different stressful situations and decide what particular methods are useful in coping with those situations. A careful study of these situations will enable you to become more fully acquainted with stress reduction methods.

The twenty methods for controlling stress have been discussed one at a time in an order that makes it possible to get to know them well. In actual stressful situations you will not make use of all methods at once, nor will you necessarily use them in the order discussed. Usually the attitudes discussed in Part I are the beginning of any stress control program, but often seeking support, while presented last in this guide, is the first step to take. You will find it useful, therefore, to see how the methods for controlling stress are applied in specific situations.

This unit describes stressful situations experienced by three people. (The situations were written by my academic assistant, Deborah Penner.) As you read each situation, take note of what methods you would suggest for that person and then compare your suggestions to those given in the guide. While no two people would pick exactly the same combinations of methods for any particular situation, you can use the discussion here to get some idea of how well you understand how to apply the methods in actual situations.

As you read this unit, bear in mind that the methods for stress control are designed to help a person deal with the stress which comes from problems and difficulties that he faces; they are not intended to be solutions for the problems themselves. Also, recall some of the ideas about the methods that were discussed in the introduction to this guide. Some of the steps to be taken in dealing with stressful situations will seem obvious—yet we often forget to do what is obvious to others. My experience in working with groups indicates that applying the methods to stressful situations for purposes of illustration sometimes seems mechanical and easy. In actual situations, however, as you use the methods, it need not be mechanical at all. And, as you have probably already noted, changing attitudes, revising unspoken rules, setting priorities, or using the other methods is not easy, but well worth the effort.

BOB—THE SITUATION

Bob is an executive for an insurance company in New York City, where he has been the head of his department for seven years. This afternoon, he is in his office, sitting at his desk, brooding, having canceled his lunch engagement. An hour ago he got back from a conference with his boss, who told him, in no uncertain terms, that he's not been pleased with Bob's recent performance on the job. He says Bob seems agitated, edgy, and is obviously not concentrating on his work. He's concerned because several of the members of Bob's department have spoken to him quite negatively about the changes they've noticed in Bob recently. Bob feels devastated by his boss's remarks, because he'd always taken extreme pride in his work. He's embarrassed and angry at himself for "falling below par," as he puts it. "What will people think of me if I can't do any better than this?" He's also angry at the others in his office for talking to his boss about him and feels that much of the trouble is their fault, anyway, not his.

However, when Bob is honest with himself, he knows the reason that the office hasn't been running as smoothly as it should is partly his responsibility, although he hadn't realized the extent to which his personal life had been interfering with his work. While he thinks his boss might have been exaggerating the problem a little bit, there is no denying the fact that Bob is extremely upset and agitated. He's having marital problems which are making him tense and tired. From a comfortable life in which his career success was balanced neatly by his wife's full-time support as homemaker, his family life has abruptly changed course.

At age thirty-nine, after fourteen years of marriage and three children, Cheryl, his wife, has resumed her career in market research. Quite unexpectedly, Bob feels their relationship has changed completely. He thinks, "I counted on her always being there, just like before—supportive, adjusting to my needs." Although he is proud of Cheryl's accomplishments and grateful for her financial contribution, he is impatient with the demands of her new job and resents her newfound independence. He feels like less of a man somehow. Cheryl doesn't seem like the same person he married. She's moved off into a whole new world, and he cannot understand why. He thinks, "I just can't stand the way she is now. Why is she doing this to me and the children?"

Bob had always been the breadwinner and the "provider" for his wife and children. He thinks, "I was the sole support of the family, and now, if I died, she could get along fine without me!" He feels her returning to work was a spur-of-the-moment decision; he never remembers her even talking about it before. She seemed perfectly satisfied to raise their children and be his wife. Now he feels she doesn't need him anymore. "Isn't that what marriage is all about anyway?" he asks himself. Each person is supposed to hold up his end of the bargain, and she's not fulfilling her part of the contract anymore. He really believes she's being unfair. Also, the two of them seem to argue with increasing regularity, although Bob never brings up the subject of what's really bothering him. He thinks, "We never used to disagree about little things as we do now. This new job of hers is ruining us!"

Bob sees all of this as threatening to their relationship. He feels hurt when Cheryl has no time to listen to what went on at his office, yet can't seem to express any of these feelings to anyone, especially to her. He also believes she's shirking her duties as a mother. His children are eight, nine, and eleven years old, and he feels they need a mother at home. He gets angry at her (though he tries not to show it directly) because he feels she should understand him without his having to say anything. After all, they should know each other pretty well by now, shouldn't they? They've been married for fourteen years. When it comes right down to it, he'd just rather not say anything. He's restless, frustrated, and is beginning to wonder if it's even worth continuing the marriage. For all he knows, she's probably even considering that herself. Maybe she's even found someone else. This possibility is particularly worrisome for Bob.

BOB—APPLYING THE METHODS

How can Bob use the methods described in this guide to help him cope with his stress? Remember that these methods are aimed at helping Bob deal with his inner reaction to his difficulties and are not intended to resolve his problems for him. While he is using other resources to deal with his work and his marriage, he can use stress control methods to help him through this very difficult time.

If Bob *takes inventory*, he will discover that his current stress revolves around two basic parts of his life: (1) demands he places on himself and others; and (2) a series of unspoken rules that he has for his marriage. He wants to work so well all the time that he never receives criticism from others. He has difficulty in recognizing that he can be a good worker without doing everything perfectly. Being sensitive to criticism, he in effect demands that others not criticize him and is angered when they do. He also has a number of unspoken rules about marriage, such as:

My wife must be home to support me emotionally.
I am a man only when I am the sole breadwinner.
My wife must be financially dependent on me.
My wife must know what I want without my telling her.
A man must have others needing him.

Once Bob realizes that these demands and rules contribute to his current stress, he can begin to see that, rather than being a passive victim in this situation, he too is responsible for how he feels. When he accepts responsibility for the part he is playing in his difficulties, he is starting to *assume control*. He can begin to ask, "What can I do about my reactions to these circumstances," and in so doing, he adopts a *problem-solving approach* instead of sitting in his office and brooding. Perhaps he could also see that the situation he is in is not that unusual; indeed, *stress is a part of life*. He can learn to give up some of his self-imposed demands, revise his understanding of what marriage is all about, and thus use *stress for growth*. Had Bob done some of this growing earlier in his life, he would have been able to *anticipate change;* then, perhaps, his wife's decision to return to work would not have seemed so unreasonable.

Given this understanding of Bob's situation, we can see that, once he adopts the important attitudes just discussed, he will profit most by *reducing demand*, particularly self-imposed demands, learning to accept himself even when he does not live up to all his demands, and *revising his unspoken rules*. He can first challenge those rules and then revise them to read something like this:

I prefer it when my wife is at home, but she has the right to a fulfilling life too.
I like being the breadwinner and having others dependent on me, but I can stand it even when I'm not; I can be a man even when my wife is not completely dependent on me.

Bob's feeling of being helpless and victimized will change as he adopts more constructive attitudes toward his situation and when he revises his unspoken rules. He can also *assume control* by being more *assertive:* why not make his feelings and needs known to his wife? Control also comes when we *seek information:* if he is wondering whether his wife considers the marriage worth continuing, he can discuss it with her. Doing so would not only help him feel more in control but would also help him *reduce uncertainty*. Of course, he may not be sure, once he has talked with his wife, what the future will bring; in which case he can learn to *tolerate uncertainty*. He can also reduce his uncertainty by talking with his wife about her career and what it means to her. There is no reason for him to remain ignorant of this important part of his wife's life.

Bob also has some unfinished business in the form of unexpressed feelings. He can utilize some of the methods to *finish unfinished business* discussed in this guide, and he can also *seek support* and share these feelings with a good friend. In particular, he can find support by talking with men who have faced similar situations and thus *share in others' experience.*

When Bob finds himself especially upset and anxious about the future, he can *use a stress antidote.* He will have to word it for himself, but it might sound something like this:

> **This is a difficult situation for me but I can handle it. My problems are real ones, but they are manageable. No matter what happens, I can go on.**

Bob needs to *take care of himself* by relaxing and letting go. Further, he can also *get away from it all* either by changing his environment or by giving *himself intrinsically rewarding experiences.*

CHERYL—THE SITUATION

Cheryl is Bob's wife, and she of course sees things from a different perspective than Bob. Actually, she feels quite pleased about the new turn her life has taken. She is enjoying the excitement of being back at work and finds that her fears about returning and not being able to compete with the younger people in the business were completely unfounded. In fact, she often even becomes angry at these first- and second-year assistants because she feels they patronize her. Just because she's forty-five years old and has been "at home" for fourteen years does not mean she's forgotten everything she ever knew, nor does it mean she has to have each new detail explained three times. She wishes they would change their attitude. On the whole, however, Cheryl is still glad to be back at work. She's seeing a lot of old friends and business acquaintances whom she's been out of touch with for several years and is enjoying getting reacquainted with them and discussing the more detailed changes which have taken place in her area of marketing since she left. While she's tried to keep up with new developments at home, she still finds it a little difficult to get back into the old pattern.

Although her job at the office is running relatively smoothly, some problems at home have developed. While her children seem to be adjusting to her new life style quite well, her husband is not adjusting at all. Cheryl senses his anger and hostility directed toward her all the time, yet she doesn't know what to do for him. Whenever she tries to talk to him, he closes up. He won't even discuss *what* it is exactly that he's angry about, which Cheryl finds incredibly frustrating. She's sure it has something to do with her job. She's tried to make him feel better, but somehow, whatever she does is wrong. She tries to be cheerful all the time, but she just can't seem to make Bob happy. Consequently, she feels that she is a failure as a helper and, to some extent, as a wife.

CHERYL—APPLYING THE METHODS

From the perspective of stress management, Cheryl's situation is not very complicated. The two major sources of stress for her are the patronizing attitude of the younger people at her job and her husband's response to her work, combined with her inability to cheer him up. Cheryl can respond to her younger co-workers if she *accepts* the fact that attitudes such as theirs are *part of life*. The attitudes of other people can't always be as one would like. Further, if Cheryl can learn to *be assertive*, she can respond to them appropriately and nonaggressively. While she can accept the fact that they are patronizing, she also accepts the fact that she must do something about it. Instead of hoping and wishing they will change, she *adopts an attitude of responsibility* and sees this as her *problem to be solved*.

On the other hand, perhaps Cheryl must *reject the unreasonable demand* that she make her husband Bob feel better. She has tried to help him and done what she could, but she cannot expect to do for him what he must do for himself. If she decides that her goal is to do all she can to help him feel better (but not to *make* him feel better), she can see herself as a success and not a failure when she evaluates her efforts by seeing what she has done, not what Bob's response is.

JANET—THE SITUATION

Janet is a freshman at a small college in New England. Today marks the end of her fourth week at school. (She thinks as she walks up the path to her dorm, "What a month; it seems like I've been here forever.") Since she arrived at the place where one is supposed to spend "the four best years of one's life," the focal point of Janet's existence has been her school work. Midterms are coming up soon—Janet has four exams in three days—and she has really begun to worry about how she will do. She's found the work load at college to be much heavier than she'd expected. In high school, she was one of the top students in her class. She feels she needs to continue doing well, and now, because the courses are so much more difficult, she feels she must study all the time.

Her roommate doesn't understand her. Janet is up at 5 a.m. and doesn't go to bed sometimes until 12 a.m. This in itself wouldn't be so bad, but whenever Janet's not eating or sleeping, she has her nose in a book. Janet knows she's studying a lot, and she also knows that other students may not do as well in college as they did in high school, but she feels she is an exception and must perform in accordance with her previous standards.

Janet worries about her approach toward her school work. She knows she's studying a lot, but asks herself, "Am I taking notes correctly? Do I spend enough time on my homework? Perhaps I'm not working hard enough to do well on my midterms." She just doesn't know what is expected of her, and she's afraid of approaching her professors to ask. They seem pretty aloof, and she isn't sure how kindly they would take to answering her questions.

Janet is beginning to question her ability as a student. She doesn't feel prepared for anything and also feels like everyone else probably knows more than she does. Her roommate, for instance, never seems to study. She's in chorale and plays field hockey. Janet can only assume then that she must be smart enough not to have to study.

Aside from her worries about school, Janet misses three of the most important people in her life very much—her parents and her boyfriend. She came to this college instead of one closer to home at her parent's urging. Now she's beginning to wonder if she made the right choice. Her boyfriend, Kenny, is at another school, about 200 miles away. She misses him terribly and would like to see him every weekend. He's always urging her to come up (or asking if he can come down), yet at the same time reminding her to spend a lot of time studying so that she can achieve a superior academic average. Janet is torn between spending time on her school work and being with Kenny. The one weekend they did spend together was disastrous, however. Janet spent fourteen hours traveling, and when she was with Kenny, she didn't have a good time anyway because she was worried about her work. She wonders sometimes, "Why can't life be easier? Is all this really worth it?"

JANET—APPLYING THE METHODS

Janet's situation is not at all unusual and when she completes her *inventory*, she will note that, like many other freshmen, her stress focuses on her worries about schoolwork and the loneliness that comes from not being with her parents and boyfriend. Janet can get ready to deal with her stress by *recognizing stress as part of life*: the freshman year, particularly the first few months, is a time of unusual change and pressure—certainly every student can expect this to be a difficult period. Once she sees that her experience is not that unusual, she can stop wondering why life can't be easier and *adopt a problem-solving approach.* Further, she can *use this stress for growth,* realizing that she will learn a great deal about herself and grow considerably in the months ahead.

As Janet takes a problem-solving approach, she asks herself, "What can I do to help deal with this situation?" One of the first things she can do is to *seek support:* take every opportunity to make new friends and *share in others' experience* as well as *talk it out* with them. Her college probably has upperclassmen assigned as counselors for freshmen, a counseling center, and a dean of students office, all of which make it possible for her to *utilize resources* and *seek advice and counsel.* Further, as she makes new friends and talks with other students, she will begin to lessen her feelings of loneliness. Hence, she can *satisfy her wants* for love and companionship by actively involving herself with other people.

By *doing something specific* and *seeking information* about her concerns, Janet is better able to *assume control* of her life. When she stops to think about it, she will realize that while her parents did urge her to come to college, she chose to accept their advice and is thus not a passive victim of forces beyond her control. Thus she can adopt an *attitude of responsibility* and remind herself each day that she chooses to stay at college regardless of her worries *(make choices and decisions).*

At this point Janet is ready to *take action.* She can *reduce the uncertainty* she feels by learning all she can about what types of examinations are given, the nature of the grading system, the expectations of the professors, and other pertinent information. She must realize, however, that some questions will remain unanswered and must also learn to *tolerate uncertainty.*

Janet can also *develop competencies* that will help her deal with her work. She can learn how to take notes, study effectively, read faster, use the library, and write papers. If speaking with her professors appears to be a significant problem, then she can learn to *be assertive.* As she develops each of these competencies, Janet can *utilize resources* to help her.

Janet is working so hard and worrying so much that she will soon become inefficient in her studying. She needs to take *care of herself* and to *get away from it all* once in a while. Attention to proper diet and adequate sleep is more important than she probably realizes (watch physical health). Some regular *exercise,* combined with an occasional *change in environment* and *play* or *relaxation,* will also help. Because so much of her attention is focused on herself, she might consider *developing external interests,* perhaps by volunteering some time to a local social agency or joining an organization on campus.

Janet will also need to consider reducing *self-imposed demands.* Is it absolutely necessary to get all A's? Her *unspoken rule,* **I must be a superior student at all times,** could be revised: **I will do my best and**

accept myself whatever my grades might be. Whenever her workload seems overwhelming and she feels that she will never get it all completed, Janet can *make her activities less complex* by breaking her work up into manageable units, and then she can *finish unfinished business* by *setting short-term goals* and completing her tasks one at a time. Her boyfriend is putting her into a no-win situation by insisting that she visit him regularly and yet study enough to earn a superior academic average. She can *refuse* this *unreasonable demand,* pointing out that the more time she spends with him, the less time she has for studying.

At times Janet wonders, "Is is worth it?" Questions such as these give Janet an opportunity to *clarify her values,* and while this important task cannot be accomplished easily, now is the time for Janet to think about what she wants to do with her life and the place of education in her plans.

Perhaps as you read about these three people, you thought of methods for them to use that weren't mentioned in the discussion. You may have even decided that some of the methods suggested don't seem appropriate for the situation. That is your decision. You, as an individual, can utilize the methods of stress control that appeal to you and make sense to you in your own circumstances. Experience shows that if you develop a plan of action and conscientiously apply your selection of these methods, you can significantly reduce the amount of stress you experience.